THE AUSTRALIAN
Women's W

MW01016737

the
d̶etox
cookbook

acp
books

Looking healthy and feeling good about myself are important to me... that's why every now and then I need a bit of a tune-up. Detoxing is not a flash in the pan like so many other diets, but a healthy, sensible way to help rid yourself of many of the harmful things you take into your body simply by living in the world today. And guess what? The food in this book is so delicious, it may well become food you want to eat all the time.

Pamela Clark

Food Director

contents

It's been estimated that, on average, we eat or drink about 3.75 litres of pesticides, take in five kilograms of chemical food additives and breathe in two grams of solid pollution every year.

why you need to detox

We all want to enjoy good health, unlimited energy, restful sleep and a sense of serenity. But increasingly the world around us presents us with some real challenges in realising these goals.

We may find ourselves relying on convenience food to meet our nutritional needs because we're working longer hours. Is it any wonder, then, that our freezers tend to be stocked with frozen dinners or other convenience-oriented food, or that we find ourselves dialling takeaway more often than is healthy? And, even if we try to improve our diet, buying natural produce and ingredients isn't as easy as it once was. Many supermarket shelves are stocked with foods grown or raised with the use of pesticides and antibiotics, that contain artificial additives or preservatives, or have had much of the goodness processed out of them.

At the same time, the water that comes out of our taps contains chemical contaminants, and the air we breathe is polluted with toxins from industry, transportation and even the cleaning products we use around our homes.

These all have toxic effects – the Environmental Protection Agency in the United States considers that 60 per cent of all herbicides, 90 per cent of all fungicides and 30 per cent of all insecticides are potentially carcinogenic (cancer-causing).

cleanse, energise, pamper

note Detoxing is not suitable for pregnant women or people with diabetes, kidney disease, or eating disorders. Those with any medical condition that requires regular supervision by their doctor or prescribed medication should also seek their GP's advice before embarking on any program that involves a change of eating or exercise habits.

Besides external sources, toxins in our body can result from viral or bacterial infections, or from the by-products of the metabolism of certain bacteria and yeasts that inhabit our bowel. As if this isn't enough for our bodies to deal with, nearly all of us find ourselves locked into a hyperactive state, with very little time to spend in a healing state, where we can let go of stress. We also relegate stress-beating exercise to the bottom of our to-do list.

To fight this combination of challenges, many of us turn to medical or recreational drugs to combat ills or help us unwind. But, ironically, these further pollute our bodies, causing more toxins and stress.

Unfortunately, the payoff for our 21st-century lifestyle is excess weight, allergies, headaches, fatigue, rashes, colds, coughs and a host of other ailments.

Yet there is some good news. Our body is an incredible feat of biomechanical engineering. All we need do is give it the tools – and that includes a "detox" – to repair the damage wreaked by an overload of toxins, and it will put us back onto the path to wellbeing.

What we need is a program that will cleanse and energise our body and mind, and help us build a healthy lifestyle – and that includes some self-pampering.

The benefits are many: increased energy, glowing skin, healthier hair and nails, less anxiety, better concentration, better metabolism and bowel patterns and, in the long-term, a slowing down of the ageing process and a lower risk of both minor illnesses and chronic disease.

how you know you need to detox

If you are in tune with your body, you will often feel when it is not running smoothly.

But even if you've lost touch with your personal rhythms, your body will send you plenty of signals that it needs a detox tune-up. (See the "symptoms" checklist, page 7.)

when to detox – and when not to

Detoxing can be challenging, so you need to choose a time that works for you. The start of spring, summer or autumn are best, because you don't need as much food to refuel your body as you do in winter, and detox foods tend to be light. Ideally, you should also choose a time when you're not under a lot of pressure or, better still, when you have a few days off – it's important that you take it easy.

Directly after a bout of the flu or food poisoning is a bad time to detox. So, wait until you've had sufficient time to recover.

You may also want to delay starting a detox program if you are feeling emotionally vulnerable – such as if you've just ended a relationship or moved house.

While many people choose the longer detox programs – seven days or two weeks – you should be aware that you may face some hurdles in maintaining your busy schedule. For example, you may develop a detox headache and find it difficult to concentrate. We recommend that you don't take painkillers because they add to your toxic load.

Be aware that withdrawal headaches from caffeine, which is on the "foods to avoid" list (page 10), can be particularly vicious on the second day. You'll need to make sure you drink plenty of water and that, if you want to, you can lie down until the effects of the headache subside.

If you feel light-headed on a detox program never drive a car or operate machinery. Rest is the best remedy.

Also, avoid very hot baths and showers, as these not only reduce your energy, but may increase your blood pressure.

We recommend you stop the detox program immediately if you feel sick, light-headed or dizzy, or if you have a constant headache or muscle pain that you would rate as severe. Don't feel discouraged. You can always embark on the program again when you feel more able.

do you need to detox?

How many of these symptoms apply to you?

- You're always tired and don't sleep well
- You suffer from breakouts or dull skin
- You are constipated or suffer from irritable bowel syndrome
- Your eyes are puffy and accentuated with dark circles
- You often feel nauseous or suffer from indigestion
- You have aches and pains in your joints or muscles
- You are prone to sinus problems or allergies
- You just can't get rid of cellulite
- You have skin that is dry and itchy
- Your hair is dull or greasy
- You suffer from headaches
- You suffer from night sweats
- You have bad breath
- You suffer from flatulence
- You have recurrent itchy or inflamed eyes
- Bloating and water retention are a problem for you
- You often lose your train of thought
- Your moods are up and down
- You feel anxious or depressed
- You suffer from skin rashes or eczema
- You're so stressed you want to scream

hero detox foods

apples Contain vitamin E, which improves endurance and stamina of muscles and nerves, and protects the respiratory system from toxins. Also a good source of vitamins A and C, biotin, folic acid and quercetin, an antioxidant that helps lower fat and cholesterol.

beetroot Reputed to be one of the best liver-cleansing vegetables, it also helps nourish the nervous system and brain with manganese, magnesium and folate.

broccoli Is high in folate and vitamins A and C, as well as calcium and phosphorous, which help build and maintain strong bones. It also stimulates the liver.

cabbage High in vitamin C and calcium. An excellent source of chlorine and sulphur, which expel waste and cleanse the blood.

carrots Packed with nutrients including vitamins A and C; believed to cleanse, nourish and stimulate the body, particularly the liver, kidneys and digestive system.

celery A recognised diuretic and laxative, and the richest vegetable source of sodium with more than 120mg per 100 grams.

cherries Food for the blood with iron, copper and manganese, plus vitamins A and C. They help remove toxins from the kidneys, liver and digestive system. Cherries also contain a phytochemical called ellagic acid, which could help protect against cancer.

chickpeas A good source of fibre and calcium for healthy bones, phosphorous for healthy kidneys and nerves, and potassium, which nourishes muscles.

cucumber Contains high levels of vitamin E, essential for healthy heart muscles, and iodine for healthy hair, nails, skin, teeth and thyroid function. Helps prevent water retention.

fennel A diuretic that can also help settle the stomach.

garlic A powerhouse of sulphur, a natural penicillin that helps keep the body alkaline. Garlic oil contains a substance that helps clear the respiratory and lymphatic system.

ginger Cleans, stimulates and rejuvenates the digestive system.

grapes Contain ellagic acid that may have anti-carcinogenic effects. Also contains high levels of manganese, the "memory mineral", which nourishes the nervous system, helps maintain sex hormone production and assists in the formation of healthy red blood cells. A good source of silicon, which helps circulation, prevents nervous exhaustion and is essential for healthy skin, hair and teeth.

lemons An excellent source of phosphorous, required for the repair and healthy functioning of the nervous system. Also a good source of sodium, which assists in the proper elimination of waste and cleansing of the lymphatic system, and helps stimulate the liver and gallbladder. Freshly squeezed lemon juice in warm water (ratio 25/75) first thing in the morning is a great way to pep up your liver.

melons High in sodium to help cleanse the kidneys. Also contain a host of other minerals including calcium, phosphorus, potassium, iron and zinc, as well as vitamins A and C.

onions A good source of silicon, which can promote better blood circulation and prevent nervous and mental fatigue. Also contain potent antiviral and antibacterial nutrients.

oranges Loaded with vitamin C, with an average of 30-50mg/100g of freshly squeezed juice. Also contain calcium and phosphorous and when combined, help protect the body from infections and viruses.

papaya One of the richest sources of the enzyme papain, which is essential to protein digestion. An excellent source of vitamins A and C.

parsley Stimulates the kidneys to eliminate toxic waste.

peaches A good source of vitamin A, important for healthy skin, good eyesight and protection from the effects of stress and environmental toxins. Vitamin A also protects the lungs and respiratory tract from infection. Contain sulphur, which can help expel harmful mucus from the body.

pears Contain alkaline-healing and cleansing minerals including iron, potassium, calcium, magnesium and manganese. Also contain sodium, which not only benefits the lymphatic system, but is required regularly for proper elimination of carbon dioxide waste from the lungs.

pineapples Contain bromelain, which has anti-inflammatory properties and helps the body digest protein.

sea vegetables Alginic acid, found in some seaweeds, binds with heavy metals, such as cadmium, lead, mercury and radium, to eliminate them from the body.

strawberries Contain ellagic acid that may have anti-carcinogenic effects. Weight for weight, contain 1½ times as much vitamin C as most citrus fruits and are also a good source of iron.

tomatoes Contain chlorine, an acid mineral that stimulates the liver to filter out waste products. Helps with the production of gastric juices, maintenance of correct fluid levels and reduces excess blood fat.

watercress Cleanses the blood and improves the condition of the skin.

preparing to detox

You'll notice that we've included some "day before" advice in the one-week detox menu, and some "two-days before" guidelines for the two-week program. That's because you need to ease into the program to reduce sudden withdrawal symptoms.

If you drink six cups of coffee a day and go straight onto water or herbal tea, we're pretty sure you're going to have a headache that will put you off ever undertaking a detox program again. A week before you're due to start detoxing, cut your caffeine intake by a cup a day. If you drink alcohol or eat a lot of sugar, drink or eat them less and less as the days to your detox approach.

Setting up your environment to detox is also very important. Throw out any foods that are full of sugar, caffeine, white flour or saturated and trans fats (a "bad" fat that raises cholesterol levels; usually found in cakes, biscuits and table margarines).

Ask yourself if that king-sized chocolate bar will survive your detox or whether you'll be tempted by that cup of coffee. Remember, after you've finished your detox, you'll be making healthier food choices. You'll need to replace unhealthy foods with healthy ones – lots of ruit and vegetables, filtered water, herbal teas and pulses and grains. See our menus (pp22-25) and make a shopping list. Wherever possible, buy organic so your body won't have to deal with the chemicals used on commercial fruits and vegetables.

You'll also need some essential kitchen tools: a steamer and juice extractor (borrow one if you haven't got one), for example, so you can get the benefits of freshly squeezed oranges, lemons, pineapples and more.

cleaning up

Ever wondered how the body disposes of the toxic waste accumulated in your system? Toxins are cleansed from the body in a variety of ways, but mainly through:

- your liver, for final elimination through your lungs, kidneys and intestines
- your lungs, which exhale poisonous carbon dioxide and other waste products
- your kidneys, which eliminate water-soluble toxins
- your intestines, which eliminate both water and fat-soluble toxins and wastes
- your skin, through perspiration
- your hair and nails, which eliminate some toxins, including heavy metals

In large quantities, alcohol can be a toxic substance, and heavy drinking can harm the liver and deplete nutrients such as vitamins A and C and the B-group vitamins, as well as magnesium, zinc and essential fatty acids. It can lead to severe dehydration. Modern methods of producing alcohol also means it often contains chemical pesticides, colorants and other harmful additives.

foods to avoid

Toxins are harmful substances that affect the healthy functioning of our bodies. Most people are aware that their diet needs improving and, by controlling what they eat, they can control some of the toxins that enter their body.

Most people who detox should also cut out meat, wheat and dairy. Naturopaths believe these foods create acid toxins that, in excess, can damage organs and glands, harm joints and arteries, and even inhibit immune responses.

Unfortunately, many dairy foods and meats now contain growth promoters, hormones and antibiotics that put a strain on the whole body. However, one exception is natural live yogurt, which has a soothing and nurturing effect on the digestive system, and can help keep healthy bacteria in the gut. We use sheep- or goats-milk yogurt in our recipes, as these are much easier to digest and can aid digestive disorders and stimulate digestion.

Meat is hard to digest, and is a major source of saturated fat, the kind that contributes to blocked arteries, increasing the risk of heart disease.

You'll notice we don't include fish in our detox programs, because it can harbour unwanted pollutants. But, even though we want you to stick to a vegetarian diet while cleansing and re-energising your body, you may want to incorporate fish later into your diet, and so we have included fish in the "before & after" section of the menus. In fact, most health experts recommend that you eat three servings of fish a week because of its ability to reduce the risk of heart disease, and auto-immune and joint problems.

Wheat is on the "foods to avoid" list beacuse it is a common allergen and wheat bran can inhibit the absorption of some important nutrients, as well as irritate the intestinal lining.

Bad news for cappuccino addicts: caffeine is also off limits, as are sugar and salt. Consuming an excessive amount of caffeine can result in insomnia, headaches and high blood pressure, as well as reducing the body's ability to absorb vitamins and minerals.

Of course, large amounts of refined sugar not only upset the balance of blood sugars in the body, but are full of empty kilojoules.

Salt is necessary to maintain normal hydration of the body's circulation and cellular fluids. However, many people eat too much salt, simply because food manufacturers tend to add salt to everyday foods such as bread, cereals and canned goods. Too much salt overloads the kidneys and can cause fluid retention, which may lead to heart failure, stroke, osteoporosis or kidney problems, including kidney stones.

In our detox recipes, we've used fresh herbs and lemon juice to add zest to food. We're sure you'll also find these healthier alternatives just as flavoursome.

getting the balance right

The acid/alkaline level of the body (also known as the "Ph" level) is important for healthy cells and tissues. For the body to function properly, it needs to keep its acid/alkaline balance within normal levels. If the body is too acid or too alkaline, cells can be damaged and tissues won't function effectively, thereby affecting your health.

Foods can affect the Ph level of the body (which is normally slightly alkaline), appears to be one of the causes of an unbalanced Ph level. Some foods break down into acid-forming substances, while others break down into alkaline-forming substances. The diet of many people in Western countries consists of acid-forming food (saturated fats, sugar, meat, processed foods and refined products), therefore the body has a more acid Ph level than is healthy.

Your diet should be made up of 70 per cent alkali-forming foods and 30 per cent acid-forming foods. Alkaline-forming foods consist of most fresh fruits, including citrus, melons, pineapple, mango, kiwifruit

The following are "toxins-on-a-plate": chemical preservatives, flavouring agents, additives, dyes, artificial sweeteners and hydrogenated vegetable oils. Ensure to avoid them. Also avoid processed and refined foods that have had their natural nutrients stripped and destroyed. Wherever possible, a better choice is organic whole foods.

Rather than use salt, a better way to flavour foods and give it zest, is to add fresh herbs and lemon juice.

and papaya, and vegetables, including asparagus, celery, spinach, carrot, onion, broccoli and potatoes (with the skin on). Acid-forming foods include meats, fish, poultry, eggs, cheese, bread, rice, oats, most cereals, lentils, sugar, walnuts and hazelnuts.

Naturopaths believe that keeping your body in an alkaline state will improve your mood, energy levels, sleep quality, and reduce aches and pains, headaches and, in the long-term, your risk of chronic disease.

Exercise also can affect the acid/alkaline balance of your body by making the blood more acidic. Deep breathing, on the other hand, makes the blood more alkaline.

h2o

Sixty per cent of your body is made up of fluid, which is absolutely essential for the healthy functioning of your entire system. Fluids promote chemical reactions, lubricate joints, transport nutrients and are important for kidney and immune function, healthy skin, and even the prevention of pain.

You need to drink 1-1.5 litres of pure water a day. You can add a squeeze of lemon juice to it if you wish. And you'll find plenty of delicious juices included in the detox plans.

exercise and detox

True or false. If you swim, go for a run or have a workout at the gym, you will detox faster.

False. In fact, indulging in this sort of strenuous exercise while you're on a detox program could land you in hospital. A detox is not the time to run a marathon.

No matter what detox program you choose to undertake, it's important you get plenty of rest. If you're on the one-day detox program, the most strenuous thing you should do is have a massage.

the detox cookbook

If you choose the weekend detox, a bit of gentle walking is the only exercise recommended. For the one- and two-week detox programs, two gentle walks a week are all you need to help eliminate toxins such as urea and lactic acid.

An alternative to walking is five or 10 minutes of gentle exercise, such as yoga, tai chi and chi gong. These exercises gently pump lymph, an alkaline fluid that removes acid waste from the blood and tissues, around the body. Gentle exercise also helps dissolve and eliminate crystalline acid deposits in the joints.

pamper yourself

While you're cleansing your inside with detoxing foods and juices, it's the ideal time to cleanse and pamper your outside, too.

dry body brushing and an Epsom salts bath

Dry body brushing is a stimulating therapy. It's a great detoxing treatment because it helps rid the skin of dry, dead cells and improves blood and lymph circulation. That means it helps your body dispose of some of the internal toxins being mobilised by your detox program.

You'll need a natural bristle brush or a hemp mitt. Undress then, on dry skin, use long, upward sweeping movements, starting at your feet and working up your legs and across your hips and bottom (the strokes should be towards your heart). From there, run the brush in a clockwise motion over your stomach then gently rub over your decolletage area and down your arms to your fingers.

Don't brush your breasts, face or throat, and be careful not to rub your skin too hard. Rough scrubbing can break tiny capillaries, not to mention leave you red and raw.

After you've finished dry brushing you can have a shower, or you may want to run a warm bath and put in one to two cups of Epsom salts – available from chemists or supermarkets. These contain magnesium, a mineral required for nearly all the body's cellular

Using beautiful plates, glasses and cutlery during a detox can also increase your sense of pampering yourself.

some essential oils & their uses

- bergamot – relieves stress, depression and fatigue
- cedarwood – comforting, helps calm the nerves
- chamomile – calms the nerves
- clary sage – helps relieve stress, tension and mild anxiety
- eucalyptus – can help relieve cold and flu symptoms
- fennel – detoxifying, good for digestive problems, tiredness
- frankincense – helps bring comfort
- geranium – helps calm the nerves, relieves anxiety and tension
- grapefruit – detoxifying, uplifting
- ginger – warming and stimulating
- juniper – calming and detoxifying
- lavender – helps relieve insomnia, nervous tension and headache
- lemon – helps relieve the symptoms of colds
- lime – refreshing and reviving
- myrrh – has anti-inflammatory properties
- orange – helps relieve stress and tension
- peppermint – clears the head, good for fatigue
- rosemary – uplifting and focusing
- sandalwood – warming and grounding
- tea tree – cleansing, uplifting and refreshing
- ylang ylang – a sedative, calms the nerves

activity, and is especially important to healthy muscle function.

An Epsom salts bath will stimulate lymph drainage and draw toxins out through the pores on the skin. For maximum detoxing benefits, soak about 20 minutes. Afterwards, it is recommended that you drink plenty of water and relax for an hour, as an Epsom salts bath can be quite draining.

For best results, take an Epsom salts bath every three days during a detox program. However, you shouldn't have one if you suffer from a skin condition, or have any cuts.

aromatherapy

There are few more luxurious ways to help you detox, as well as stimulate your senses, revive your soul and heal your mind and body, than aromatherapy.

While many people might think of aromatherapy simply as a form of treatment that involves nice-smelling oils, it is much more than that. The plant-extracted essential oils really do have therapeutic effects. They also can be dangerous if used incorrectly or in the wrong amounts, so always follow the instructions.

The easiest ways to use aromatherapy oils are in an oil burner or a bath. Using an oil burner is an ideal accompaniment to any relaxation or meditation that you may perform during your detox. Fill the oil-burner dish with water and light the candle. Add about five drops of essential oil to the water (some oils are not suitable for a burner, so check the label before use), and within minutes the aroma from the heated oil will gradually permeate the room.

An aromatherapy bath can feel like a luxurious treat while acting as a great tonic for the body, and the steam from the bath carries more aroma molecules to your nose than when you burn them.

The best way to use essential oils in the bath is to add them a drop at a time, using no more than six to eight drops in a full bath. Don't add more if you can't smell them after a while; they're still working. Also, don't have the water too hot or you may feel light-headed. For the same reason, saunas and steam rooms are not recommended during a detox, although they can be helpful later to keep the body healthy by helping to eliminate toxins.

As you rest in the bath your muscles relax and release lactic acid; your pores open and release toxins in the form of sweat; and your digestive system is stimulated by the heat of the bath. Your open pores allow the essential oil to penetrate your skin more readily. Try one of the essential oil blends (page 17), for a relaxing detox bath.

massage

For a pleasurable way to knead toxins from the tissues, promote lymph drainage, stimulate glandular secretions and calm the nervous system, try one of the many types of massage. It can relieve tension, help improve the immune system, tone the skin and muscles, and improve the appearance of skin, especially in areas prone to cellulite.

Book a treatment before you start your detox program, but take time to consider which style of massage will suit you best.

You may find a gentle Swedish massage is as much as you feel up to. Or, maybe a deeper therapy, such as remedial massage, is just what you need to get circulation going.

Other options include shiatsu massage, which involves stretching, manipulation and acupressure and can be quite painful (but effective), and kahuna massage, an energetic process that helps connect body and soul.

You can also massage yourself – or at least the parts you can reach. All massage strokes should be towards your heart, pushing the blood around your body in conjunction with the circulation, not against it.

Self-massage isn't quite as relaxing as having someone else do it for you, though. So why not spoil yourself? After all, you are taking time out for you.

If you feel you need extra sleep, or you simply want to lie down, it is important you follow your body's cues. Lounge around at home, if possible, assign household tasks to someone else, and try to avoid attending social functions. The whole idea is to let your body restore and regenerate.

note All essential oils must be used with caution. Some oils should be avoided by people with certain medical conditions or skin sensitivities, and by those who are pregnant. If you are unsure whether you can use essential oils, it is important to first talk to a qualified naturopathic practitioner or GP. Never take essential oils internally.

breathing

If you are what you eat, you're also a product of how you breathe. In fact, learning to breathe properly is an essential part of any self-healing detox program. If the body does not expel sufficient carbon dioxide, toxins build up.

Deep, rhythmic breathing enhances oxygenation of the blood and tissues, switching the nervous system into healing mode. By contrast, shallow, overbreathing can put you in a state of anxiety that can lead to ill health.

Try this simple breathing exercise to de-stress and recharge: sit comfortably or lie down. Place your hands gently on your stomach, with your fingertips touching. Close your eyes and take a few normal breaths while you say the word "calm" in your mind.

Now, breathe in through your nose, very slowly, to a count of four. As you inhale, push your belly up and out. Hold your breath for five counts, then gently exhale through your mouth to a count of eight. Repeat this process up to 10 times.

facials

Oh-oh. It's day two of your detox and you look like a teenager again. Don't worry. Breaking out during a cleansing program is normal. And once you've detoxed your body, skin problems should subside. To help your skin clear up, and to add extra relaxation to your detox regime, consider having a facial.

If you decide to visit a salon, make sure you choose somewhere with a relaxing atmosphere. Ask what the treatment includes before you book to make sure it will fit in with your regime. A head or shoulder massage or being left alone with a mask on for 15 minutes are both pluses because they help you relax and give you time for reflection.

If you'd prefer to treat yourself at home, stock up on some of your favourite cleanser, mask and moisturiser products before you start your detox. Or, for a natural treatment, raid the pantry. The kitchen is the ideal place for facial ingredients – you can't go past honey, natural yogurt or oatmeal. Also try your local chemist or health-food store for supplies. These are ideal places to seek out chemical-free beauty products.

A facial sauna is a good way to prepare your face for facial masks. (You should not use facial saunas if you have sensitive skin, are pregnant or suffer from asthma.) Give these facial saunas a try.

Fill a large glass bowl with 1 litre (4 cups) of near boiling water and add ingredients according to your skin type: **normal skin** add 6 drops mandarin essential oil and 2 tablespoons loose lavender tea; **oily skin** add 6 drops eucalyptus essential oil and 2 tablespoons loose lemon tea; **dry skin** add 6 drops rose essential oil and 2 tablespoons loose chamomile tea. Place a towel over your head and hold it over the bowl from a distance of about 30cm for a period of 2 minutes. Close your eyes and breathe normally; allow the steam to open your pores. Remove your face from the sauna; pat face with a warm face washer.

Ideally, perform home treatments when you are alone and have some private time and space – and don't forget to take the phone off the hook. It's all about self-pampering; an indulgence to build into your life, even after you finish your detox program.

essential oil bath blends

- To soothe aching muscles, boost the immune and digestive systems and bring a sense of peace and harmony, mix three drops of lavender, two drops of geranium and one drop of clary sage into bath.
- To boost the immune system and bring clarity to the mind, mix two drops of eucalyptus, two drops of tea tree, two drops of geranium and one drop of clary sage into bath.
- To quiet a busy brain, mix one drop of chamomile, two drops of lavender, two drops of bergamot and one drop of sandalwood into bath.

Mix your own essential oil bath blend to soothe aching muscles, boost the immune and digestive systems and bring a sense of peace and harmony.

Drink like a fish during your detox. but make it nothing but juice, water and herbal tea.

Get rid of negative emotions; laugh more, be more patient, talk about your emotions rather than bottle them up.

herbal teas

Herbal teas are no longer the brew of choice only for health fanatics or those who are vehemently anti-caffeine. These calming, reviving and healing teas have become more mainstream as an ever-increasing number of people discover their exotic flavours and soothing medicinal qualities.

The result is that it is easier than ever to order a herbal tea at a chic cafe, or to buy some – not just at specialised tea shops or health-food stores, but also in supermarkets.

There are literally hundreds of different blends you can experiment with – if you do buy your tea from a specialist shop, ask the staff to suggest something to suit your tastes and needs.

Meanwhile, here are a few suggestions to get you started:

If you're looking for a vitamin C boost, brew yourself some **rosehip tea**. Vitamin C can help strengthen your immune system and it's also vital for anti-ageing.

Raspberry tea is also a good source of vitamin C. It can be used as a blood purifier and tonic as well as help control diarrhoea. It can also help in reducing painful menstruation.

Strawberry leaf tea is believed to help soothe stomach troubles and eczema.

Tea made with **thyme** can help improve your immune system as well as promote perspiration, both ideal during a detox.

After dinner, a **peppermint tea** can stimulate digestion, while **camomile tea** helps soothe the stomach and nerves to prepare you for a good night's sleep.

Dandelion tea is an effective diuretic that can also help improve liver function.

Lemon balm tea can help lift your spirits.

Teas containing **chaparral, schisandra and St Mary's thistle** are all potent ways to treat toxic poisoning of the body.

detoxing your emotions

For a detox to work on all aspects of your life, you need to do more than cleanse your body. you need to detox your emotions.

Holistic healers believe that old resentments can burden your body and deplete your energy and, surprisingly, this idea is slowly becoming more accepted by practioners of traditional medicine.

That's because there is increasing evidence that emotions create chemical reactions in the body, and that these substances, which have the potential to cause health problems later, can be stored in muscles and organs.

This area of "emotional" science is called neuroscience or "bodymind" medicine. While much more research is needed into the field, there is no doubt that holding onto anger, resentment, frustration or envy can wear down your mind and body.

If nothing else, you will regularly feel fatigued and have a diminished capacity to enjoy your everyday life. Emotional detoxing means not only addressing these old "wounds", but also any harmful thought patterns and habits leading to fear and anxiety – both of which can impact on your health.

So take some time during your detox program to sit quietly and think about what negative emotions you regularly feel, or what negative thoughts consistently run through your mind.

You may decide that you need to learn to laugh more, to be more patient with others – or yourself – to talk about your emotions rather than bottle them up – or even to give up being a perfectionist.

At the same time, you may want to let go of old hurts or disappointments that prevent you being healthy and happy. It may be a simple matter of forgiving others – or yourself – for what is in the past, or simply accepting something the way it is.

A simple ceremony, such as burning a letter in which you have written the feelings or experiences you want to shed, or spending

possible side effects of detoxing

- Unfair as it may seem, some people get next to no detoxing symptoms. However, most people will notice some annoying side effects, and these will also vary greatly from person to person.
- Detoxing symptoms commonly include headaches, lower back pain, dry mouth, coated tongue, bad breath, skin rashes, nausea, body odour, weakness, fatigue, abdominal gas and rumblings, palpitations, mucous discharges, irritability, boredom, anxiety, emotional upset, joint and muscular aches and pains, cold feet and hands, vivid dreams, sleeplessness and more. As well, existing health problems, such as arthritis, may seem to worsen initially, and the effects of old injuries may also become evident.
- The first three or four days is the most common time for reactions and withdrawal symptoms to occur, so it's naturally the most difficult time. But if you find you can put up with mild-to-moderate side effects, don't get discouraged – keep going.
- However, as previously advised, if you feel light-headed or dizzy, have a level of headache or muscle pain you rate as severe, or develop a rash you don't think is normal, stop the detox program immediately and see your doctor. Otherwise, any unpleasant side effects will eventually settle down.

Remember, it's about self-pampering, something to gradually build into your life even after you finish your detox program.

20 minutes a day during detox in quiet meditation, may be all the emotional medicine you need.

However, if you discover some deep emotional issues that you think you need help in dealing with, seek the support of a therapist or counsellor after your detox to help you achieve a state of wellness and fulfilment. Remember, one of the aims of a detox is to learn how to look after yourself using healthy food, regular exercise and self-pampering. Practising positive self-talk and addressing toxic emotions should be part of your resolve to stay well.

Why not make it a regular habit to spend 30 minutes a day relaxing and detoxing your mind?

eating out during detox

If you choose to go to a restaurant while you're detoxing, you probably possess a will of iron. After all, you'll need to avoid the wine list, the dessert menu and many of the entrees or mains that don't fit in with your cleansing program. That said, if you really want to eat out, here are some tips to help you avoid falling off the detox wagon.

First, tell your dining companions that you are on a detox program rather than make excuses about why you're not having a glass of wine, or passing on the tiramisu.

Second, you may need to tell the waiter that you don't want butter, oil or salt added to your food. Choose a salad on the menu, without any dressing, or a vegetarian entree or main. And don't be afraid to ask how the meals have been prepared, or to request that certain ingredients be omitted.

Bottled water is a good drink choice, but you may find that the restaurant is also happy to prepare a fresh juice.

Enjoy the company of friends, rather than concentrating on the food, and you'll find eating out is not as daunting as it sounds.

coming out of detox

It's important to ease your body out of a detox program. That's why we've included a "day after" menu in the one-week and two-week detoxes. After you've gone through these menus, continue on the straight and narrow with a healthy, varied diet based on the key foods found in the detoxing menus.

Try not to over-exert yourself and, if possible, don't rush straight back to anything that will cause you stress. Don't be surprised if you feel different emotionally as well as physically – remember, you've cleared out toxins that have been weighing down your body and mind.

after detox

Keep your pantry and fridge stocked with the natural, energy-giving foods you enjoyed on your detox. Buy in-season fruit and vegetables to get maximum nutritional benefit and, if possible, buy organic.

Remember, stress is one of the major contributors to a toxic state of health, so build pampering and healing routines into your daily life as well. And don't forget to spend some time each day detoxing negative emotions.

After your detox, we strongly recommend you begin and maintain a regular exercise program. Exercise improves circulation, so your body can carry oxygen and expel wastes more effectively; enhances your sense of wellbeing; helps control your appetite and your weight; and de-stresses your body. Without exercise the adrenalin you produce in a hyperactive state has no outlet and can harm muscles, joints and organs.

You don't need to pound the pavements. While you're detoxing, make a plan to learn Pilates, yoga, tai chi or other gentle forms of exercise that treat the body and the mind. Other ideas for fun exercise include hiking, abseiling, trampolining, rollerblading, skiing, cycling and dancing.

What we can aim for is to take some of the healthy dietary habits we learned during our detox into our everyday life, and add relaxation and exercise programs to keep our body and mind healthy.

Ideally, everyone who goes on a detox would continue to live an idyllic lifestyle that was so healthy they'd never need to detox again.

cleanse, energise, pamper

21

menu plans

one day mono detox menu plan

This can be a good way to introduce yourself to the idea of detox. It's simple: you just eat one type of raw fruit or vegetable for the entire day. The food most commonly chosen is grapes, but you may also like to consider apples, pears, carrots or even papaya. Make sure you eat lightly the night before your one-day detox, and get plenty of rest. note Don't go mad the next day – ease out of your detox gently with a light, healthy diet.

BREAKFAST	MORNING TEA	LUNCH	AFTERNOON TEA	DINNER
Hot lemon water p118 Grapes or grape juice (or your chosen fruit or vegetable)	Grapes or grape juice (or your chosen fruit or vegetable) Filtered water	Grapes or grape juice (or your chosen fruit or vegetable) Filtered water	Grapes or grape juice (or your chosen fruit or vegetable) Filtered water or herbal tea p18	Grapes or grape juice (or your chosen fruit or vegetable) Filtered water or herbal tea p18

one weekend detox menu plan

note Juices should be no larger than 250ml. You should always rinse your mouth or clean your teeth after drinking citrus juices as they're acid and could damage your teeth enamel.

BREAKFAST	MORNING TEA	LUNCH	AFTERNOON TEA	DINNER
-	-	-	-	*The night before* Mixed bean salad p33
Day 1 Hot lemon water p118 Peach, apple and strawberry juice p42 Papaya with passionfruit and lime p113	Watermelon and mint juice p46	Lamb's lettuce salad with pecans and orange p91	Watercress, beetroot and celery juice p42	Asian broth p62
Day 2 Hot lemon water p118 Orange and ginger juice p45 Mango cheeks with lime wedges p116	Pineapple, orange and strawberry juice p46	Green vegetable salad with american mustard dressing p88	Ginger tea p122	Stir-fried asian greens with tofu p70

seven-day detox menu plan

BREAKFAST	MORNING TEA	LUNCH	AFTERNOON TEA	DINNER
The day before Apple and blueberry muesli p34	-	White bean salad p29	-	Vegetable stir-fry served with steamed brown rice p34
Day 1 Hot lemon water p118 Mixed berry juice p45 Four-fruit combo p112	Watermelon and mint juice p46	Orange, fennel and almond salad p91	Beetroot, carrot and spinach juice p46	Roasted cherry tomatoes, broccolini and pepitas p73
Day 2 Hot lemon water p118 Strawberry and papaya juice p42 1 banana	Mixed berry juice p45	Spinach and zucchini salad with yogurt hummus p92	Grapes	Ratatouille p73
Day 3 Hot lemon water p118 Raspberry and peach juice p45 1 nectarine	Grapes	Greek salad p92	Silver beet, apple and celery juice p49	Black-eyed beans with kumara, shallots and garlic p74
Day 4 Hot lemon water p118 Orange, carrot and ginger juice p58 Macerated fruits p112	Watercress, beetroot and celery juice p42	Roasted tomato and capsicum soup p63	Strawberry, honey and soy smoothie p49	Stir-fried asian greens with mixed mushrooms served with steamed brown rice p82
Day 5 Hot lemon water p118 Mango and grapefruit juice p50 Cherries and yogurt p117	½ mango	Potato and bean salad with lemon yogurt dressing p95	Mint tea p122	Roasted vegetable stack p74
Day 6 Hot lemon water p118 Peach, apple and strawberry juice p42 Apple and blueberry muesli p34	Pineapple, ginger and mint juice p53	Vegetable soup pg 54 Lamb's lettuce salad with pecans and orange p91	Carrot dip with crudités p86	Pearl barley salad p96
Day 7 Hot lemon water p118 Pear and ginger juice p57x Macerated fruits p112	Orange, carrot and ginger juice p58x	Dhal with vegetables p77	Beetroot, carrot and spinach juice p46	Pan-fried tofu with vietnamese coleslaw salad p95
The day after Apple and blueberry muesli p34	-	Salad, goat cheese and pecan sandwich p30	-	Steamed asian bream p37

two-week detox menu plan

BREAKFAST	MORNING TEA	LUNCH	AFTERNOON TEA	DINNER
Two day's before Apple and pear juice p49 Apple and blueberry muesli p34	-	Open rye sandwich p33	-	Grilled blue-eye with gai lan p41
One day before Pear and ginger juice p57 Apple and blueberry muesli p34	-	Asparagus caesar salad p26	-	Vegetable and white bean stew p41
Day 1 Hot lemon water p118 Apple and celery juice p50 Banana with passionfruit yogurt p113	Pineapple, ginger and mint juice p53	Greek salad p92	Lemon grass and kaffir lime leaf tea p121	Brown rice with vegetables and tahini dressing p77
Day 2 Hot lemon water p118 Mandarin juice p53 Apple and pear compote with dates p110	Mint tea p122	Cos, snow pea and roasted celeriac salad p96	Beetroot, carrot and spinach juice p46	Brown rice pilaf p85
Day 3 Hot lemon water p118 Ginger, orange and pineapple juice p53 Kiwi fruit, lychee and lime salad p114	Grapes	Chickpea, watercress and capsicum salad p99	Hummus with crudités p86	Baked potato with guacamole p78
Day 4 Hot lemon water p118 Grapefruit and blood orange juice p54 1 banana	Melon slices (one type)	Potato and asparagus salad with yogurt and mint dressing p99	Silver beet, apple and celery juice p49	Leek, goat cheese and brown lentil bake p78
Day 5 Hot lemon water p118 Kiwi fruit and green grape juice p54 Figs and sheep milk yogurt and honey p114	Pineapple, orange and strawberry juice p46	Borlotti bean, brown rice and almond salad p100	Cardamom and chamomile tea p121	Roasted egg tomatoes with barley salad p100
Day 6 Hot lemon water p118 Apple and pear juice p49 Banana with passionfruit p115	Strawberry, honey and soy smoothie p49	Pear, spinach, walnut and celery salad p103	Beetroot dip with crudités p87	Roasted root vegetables with yogurt p81

BREAKFAST	MORNING TEA	LUNCH	AFTERNOON TEA	DINNER
Day 7 Hot lemon water p118 Orange, carrot and celery juice p57 Apple and pear compote with dates p110	Tangelo and ginger juice p54	Leek and potato soup p64	Cinnamon and orange tea p122	Brown rice with vegetables and tahini dressing p77
Day 8 Hot lemon water p118 Mandarin juice p53 1 pear	1 custard apple	Eggplant with salsa fresca p81	Raita with crudités p87	Thai soy bean salad with grapes and pink grapefruit p103
Day 9 Hot lemon water p118 Ginger, orange and pineapple juice p53 Lychees with passionfruit pg 115	Blood plums with honey and cardamom yogurt pg 117	Soba salad with seaweed, ginger and vegetables p104	Mint tea p122	Grilled asparagus with warm tomato dressing p104
Day 10 Hot lemon water p118 Pear and grape juice p50 Stewed prunes with orange p116	Lemon grass and kaffir lime leaf tea p121	Pumpkin and kumara soup p67	Carrot dip with crudités p86	Baked beetroot salad with cannellini beans, fetta and mint p109
Day 11 Hot lemon water p118 Orange, carrot and celery juice p57 Mango cheeks with lime wedges p116	1 banana	Roasted pumpkin, pecan and fetta salad p107	Ginger tea p122	Stir-fried asian greens with mixed mushrooms p82
Day 12 Hot lemon water p118 Orange, mango and strawberry juice p57 1 cup mixed berries	Watercress, beetroot and celery juice p42	Vegetable and soba soup p67	Beetroot dip and crudités p87	Chickpea patties with tomato and cucumber salad p82
Day 13 Hot lemon water p118 Orange, carrot and ginger juice p58 Watermelon slices	Cinnamon and orange tea p122	Dhal with vegetables p77	Carrot, ginger and silver beet juice p58	Stir-fried tofu with vegetables and lemon grass p85
Day 14 Hot lemon water p118 Apple and blueberry museli p34 Melon slices	Banana soy smoothie p58	Tomato and avocado salad with tofu pesto p107	Hummus with crudités p86	Lentil and vegetable soup p68
The day after Apple and blueberry muesli p34	-	Lavash wrap p30	-	Oven-roasted ratatouille with almond gremolata p38
Two days after Porridge with poached pears and blueberries p29	-	Vegetable soup p64 Cos, snow pea and roasted celeriac salad p96	-	Poached flathead with herb salad p38

menu plans

25

asparagus caesar salad

1 slice wholemeal bread (45g),
  crust removed
1 teaspoon olive oil
½ clove garlic, crushed
170g asparagus, trimmed,
  chopped coarsely
½ baby cos lettuce (90g),
  leaves separated
caesar dressing
½ clove garlic, crushed
1 teaspoon american mustard
2 teaspoons lemon juice
2 tablespoons sheep milk yogurt
1 tablespoon water

1 Preheat oven to 180°C/160°C fan-forced.
2 Cut bread into 3cm cubes. Combine oil and garlic in small bowl, add bread; toss bread to coat in mixture. Place bread, in single layer, on oven tray; toast, uncovered, 10 minutes.
3 Meanwhile, place ingredients for caesar dressing in screw-top jar; shake well.
4 Boil, steam or microwave asparagus until just tender; drain.
5 Place croutons and asparagus in medium bowl with lettuce; toss gently to combine.
6 Serve salad drizzled with dressing.

preparation time 15 minutes **cooking time** 10 minutes **serves** 1
nutritional count per serving 9g total fat (0.8g saturated fat); 865kJ (207 cal); 19.7g carbohydrate; 10.2g protein; 6.7g fibre

before & after detox

porridge with poached pears and blueberries

white bean salad

porridge with poached pears and blueberries

¾ cup (180ml) hot water
⅓ cup (30g) rolled oats
1 small pear (180g), cored,
    chopped coarsely
½ cup (125ml) cold water
2 tablespoons frozen blueberries,
    thawed

1 Combine the hot water and oats in small saucepan over medium heat; cook, stirring, about 5 minutes or until porridge is thick and creamy.
2 Meanwhile, place pear and the cold water in small saucepan; bring to the boil. Reduce heat; simmer, uncovered, about 5 minutes or until pear has softened.
3 Serve porridge topped with pears and 1 tablespoon of the poaching liquid; sprinkle with berries.

preparation time 10 minutes cooking time 10 minutes serves 1
nutritional count per serving 2.7g total fat (0.5g saturated fat); 882kJ (211 cal); 43.4g carbohydrate; 3.9g protein 6.6g fibre

white bean salad

50g mesclun
½ cup (100g) canned white beans,
    rinsed, drained
2 tablespoons coarsely chopped
    fresh tarragon
2 tablespoons coarsely chopped
    fresh flat-leaf parsley
1 small carrot (70g), cut into matchsticks
½ lebanese cucumber (65g),
    cut into matchsticks
2 red radishes (70g), trimmed,
    cut into matchsticks
2 tablespoons fresh apple juice
1 tablespoon apple cider vinegar
1 tablespoon toasted sunflower seeds
1 tablespoon toasted pepitas

1 Place mesclun, beans, herbs, carrot, cucumber, radish, juice and vinegar in medium bowl; toss gently to combine.
2 Serve salad topped with seeds.

preparation time 15 minutes serves 1
nutritional count per serving 12.3g total fat (0.5g saturated fat); 1145kJ (274 cal); 21g carbohydrate; 10.1g protein; 12.5g fibre
tip Many varieties of pre-cooked white beans are available canned, among them cannellini, butter and haricot beans; any of these are suitable for this salad.

salad, goat cheese and pecan sandwich

40g goat milk cheese
1 tablespoon finely chopped pecans
1 tablespoon coarsely chopped
   fresh flat-leaf parsley
2 slices wholemeal bread (90g)
1 small tomato (90g), sliced thinly
½ lebanese cucumber (65g),
   sliced thinly lengthways
½ small carrot (35g), sliced thinly
   lengthways
2 small baby cos lettuce leaves

1 Combine cheese, nuts and parsley in small bowl.
2 Spread cheese mixture on each slice of bread; top one slice with tomato, cucumber, carrot and lettuce. Top with remaining slice.
preparation time 15 minutes **serves** 1
nutritional count per serving 16.5g total fat (5g saturated fat); 1593kJ (381 cal); 40.8g carbohydrate; 17.1g protein; 10.6g fibre

lavash wrap

1 slice wholemeal lavash
¼ small avocado (50g)
1 teaspoon tahini
½ cup (60g) coarsely grated
   uncooked beetroot
⅓ cup (50g) coarsely grated
   uncooked pumpkin
¼ small red capsicum (40g),
   sliced thinly
40g mushrooms, sliced thinly
¼ small red onion (25g), sliced thinly

1 Spread bread with avocado and tahini.
2 Place remaining ingredients on long side of bread; roll to enclose filling.
preparation time 15 minutes **serves** 1
nutritional count per serving 13.4g total fat (2.6g saturated fat); 1463kJ (350 cal); 45.1g carbohydrate; 12.2g protein; 10.1g fibre

salad, goat cheese and pecan sandwich

lavash wrap

open rye sandwich

mixed bean salad

open rye sandwich

1 teaspoon finely chopped fresh basil
1 teaspoon finely chopped fresh mint
1 teaspoon finely chopped fresh
   flat-leaf parsley
1 tablespoon ricotta cheese
1 slice rye bread (40g)
½ cup (10g) loosely packed
   baby rocket leaves
1 small tomato (90g), sliced thinly
½ lebanese cucumber (65g), sliced thinly
1 tablespoon alfalfa sprouts

1 Combine herbs and cheese in small bowl.
2 Spread cheese mixture on bread; top with remaining ingredients.
preparation time 10 minutes **serves** 1
nutritional count per serving 3.7g total fat (1.7g saturated fat);
635kJ (152 cal); 21.8g carbohydrate; 7.6g protein; 4.9g fibre

mixed bean salad

1 clove garlic, crushed
2 teaspoons olive oil
2 teaspoons fresh lemon juice
½ x 300g can four-bean mix,
   rinsed, drained
1 trimmed celery stalk (100g),
   chopped finely
½ medium yellow capsicum (100g),
   chopped finely
¼ cup (30g) seeded black olives,
   chopped coarsely
¼ cup loosely packed fresh flat-leaf
   parsley leaves
½ small red onion (50g), sliced thinly
1 cup (20g) loosely packed
   baby rocket leaves

1 Place garlic, oil and juice in screw-top jar; shake well.
2 Place remaining ingredients and dressing in medium bowl;
toss gently to combine.
preparation time 15 minutes **serves** 1
nutritional count per serving 10.3g total fat (1.5g saturated fat);
995kJ (238 cal); 27.6g carbohydrate; 9.3g protein; 10.5g fibre

apple and blueberry muesli

2 tablespoons rolled oats
⅓ cup (80ml) fresh apple juice
½ medium apple (75g), grated coarsely
⅓ cup (50g) blueberries
⅓ cup (95g) sheep milk yogurt
1 tablespoon fresh apple juice, extra
1 tablespoon blueberries, extra

1 Combine oats and juice in small bowl, cover; refrigerate about 1 hour or until oats soften. Stir in apple, blueberries and yogurt.
2 Serve muesli drizzled with extra juice and topped with extra blueberries.
preparation time 10 minutes (plus refrigeration time) **serves** 1
nutritional count per serving 7.2g total fat (0.2g saturated fat); 1083kJ (259 cal); 39.7g carbohydrate; 6.7g protein; 3.9g fibre

vegetable stir-fry

1 teaspoon sesame oil
100g fresh shiitake mushrooms, sliced thickly
1 medium carrot (120g), sliced thinly
2 tablespoons water
100g broccoli, sliced thinly
75g snow peas, trimmed, sliced thickly
1 tablespoon tamari
1 green onion, sliced thinly

1 Heat oil in wok; stir-fry mushroom and carrot 2 minutes. Add the water; stir-fry 5 minutes or until carrot just softens. Add broccoli and snow peas; stir-fry until broccoli is just tender. Stir in tamari.
2 Serve stir-fry topped with onion.
preparation time 10 minutes cooking time 10 minutes **serves** 1
nutritional count per serving 5.4g total fat (0.8g saturated fat); 778kJ (186 cal); 23.7g carbohydrate; 10.8g protein; 11.7g fibre

apple and blueberry muesli

vegetable stir-fry

steamed asian bream

poached flathead with herb salad

steamed asian bream

1 whole bream (240g)
3cm piece fresh ginger (15g),
  cut into matchsticks
1 green onion, sliced thinly
1 small carrot (70g), cut into matchsticks
1 tablespoon tamari
1 teaspoon sesame oil

1 Preheat oven to 200°C/180°C fan-forced.
2 Lightly oil sheet of foil large enough to enclose fish. Place fish on foil, fill cavity with half of the vegetables. Brush fish with combined tamari and oil; top with remaining vegetables.
3 Fold edges of foil to enclose fish; place fish parcel on oven tray. Cook about 15 minutes or until fish is cooked as desired.
4 Serve fish sprinkled with fresh coriander leaves, if desired.
preparation time 10 minutes **cooking time** 15 minutes **serves** 1
nutritional count per serving 11.2g total fat (2.9g saturated fat); 957kJ (229 cal); 5g carbohydrate; 26.8g protein; 2.4g fibre

poached flathead with herb salad

3 cups (750ml) water
2 cloves garlic, crushed
5cm piece fresh ginger (25g),
  sliced thinly
2 flathead fillets (220g)
1 lime, cut into wedges
herb salad
¼ cup loosely packed fresh mint leaves
¼ cup loosely packed fresh
  coriander leaves
¼ cup loosely packed fresh
  basil leaves, torn
½ small red onion (50g), sliced thinly
1 lebanese cucumber (130g),
  seeded, sliced thinly
1 tablespoon fresh lime juice
1cm piece fresh ginger (5g), grated

1 Place the water, garlic and ginger in medium frying pan; bring to the boil. Add fish, reduce heat; simmer, uncovered, about 5 minutes or until fish is cooked as desired. Remove fish with slotted spoon; discard liquid.
2 Meanwhile, combine ingredients for herb salad in medium bowl.
3 Serve fish with salad and lime wedges.
preparation time 20 minutes **cooking time** 10 minutes **serves** 1
nutritional count per serving 3g total fat (1g saturated fat); 1124kJ (269 cal); 8.3g carbohydrate; 49.6g protein; 6.6g fibre

oven-roasted ratatouille with almond gremolata

2 baby eggplants (120g),
  chopped coarsely
1 medium zucchini (120g),
  chopped coarsely
1 small red capsicum (150g),
  chopped coarsely
1 clove garlic, crushed
2 teaspoons olive oil
100g mushrooms, chopped coarsely
125g cherry tomatoes, halved
almond gremolata
2 tablespoons coarsely chopped
  fresh flat-leaf parsley
2 tablespoons coarsely chopped
  fresh basil
1 teaspoon finely grated lemon rind
2 tablespoons toasted slivered almonds,
  chopped coarsely
1 clove garlic, crushed

1 Preheat oven to 200°C/180°C fan-forced.
2 Combine eggplant, zucchini, capsicum, garlic and oil in small shallow baking dish. Roast, uncovered, 30 minutes, stirring occasionally. Add mushroom and tomato; roast, uncovered, about 10 minutes or until vegetables are just tender.
3 Meanwhile, combine ingredients for almond gremolata in small bowl.
4 Serve ratatouille topped with gremolata.
preparation time 10 minutes **cooking time** 40 minutes **serves** 1
nutritional count per serving 21.6g total fat (2.4g saturated fat); 1304kJ (312 cal); 16g carbohydrate; 13.8g protein; 14.2g fibre

grilled blue-eye with gai lan

vegetable and white bean stew

grilled blue-eye with gai lan

200g blue-eye fillet
200g gai lan, chopped coarsely
ginger and garlic dressing
2cm piece fresh ginger (10g), grated
1 clove garlic, crushed
1 tablespoon water
1 tablespoon tamari

1 Cook fish in heated lightly oiled small frying pan, uncovered, until cooked through.
2 Meanwhile, boil, steam or microwave gai lan until tender; drain.
3 Place ingredients for ginger and garlic dressing in screw-top jar; shake well.
4 Serve fish with gai lan, drizzle with dressing.
preparation time 10 minutes cooking time 10 minutes serves 1
nutritional count per serving 1.7g total fat (0.2g saturated fat); 828kJ (198 cal); 3.5g carbohydrate; 41.2g protein; 8.2g fibre

vegetable and white bean stew

1 teaspoon olive oil
1 small leek (200g), sliced thinly
1 medium carrot (120g), sliced thickly
1 shallot (25g), chopped finely
2 cloves garlic, crushed
2 tablespoons rolled oats
1½ cups (375ml) water
2 tablespoons coarsely chopped
   fresh chives
½ cup (100g) canned white beans,
   rinsed, drained
2 teaspoons finely grated lemon rind
2 tablespoons sheep milk yogurt

1 Heat oil in medium saucepan; cook leek, carrot, shallot and garlic, stirring, 10 minutes. Add oats and the water; bring to the boil. Reduce heat; simmer, covered, about 15 minutes or until liquid is almost absorbed. Stir in half of the chives.
2 Mash beans with rind and yogurt in small saucepan; cook, stirring, until heated through.
3 Serve stew topped with bean mixture and remaining chives.
preparation time 15 minutes cooking time 30 minutes serves 1
nutritional count per serving 9.2g total fat (0.9g saturated fat); 1120kJ (268 cal); 32.9g carbohydrate; 12.7g protein; 13.8g fibre

All juices have a preparation time of 5 minutes and serve 1.

peach, apple and strawberry

We used a green apple in this recipe, but you can use the colour of your choice.

1 medium apple (150g), cut into wedges
1 medium peach (150g), cut into wedges
2 strawberries (40g)

1 Push ingredients through juice extractor into glass; stir to combine.
nutritional count per serving 0.3g total fat; (0g saturated fat); 451kJ (108 cal); 24.3g carbohydrate; 2.2g protein; 5.1g fibre

watercress, beetroot and celery

1 trimmed celery stalk (100g), chopped coarsely
3 baby beetroots (75g), cut into wedges
50g watercress, trimmed
½ cup (125ml) water

1 Push celery, beetroot and watercress through juice extractor into glass.
2 Stir in the water.
nutritional count per serving 0.4g total fat (0g saturated fat); 222kJ (53 cal); 8.9g carbohydrate; 3.5g protein; 6g fibre

strawberry and papaya

We used the red-fleshed Hawaiian or Fijian variety of papaya in this recipe.

4 strawberries (80g)
80g papaya
½ cup (125ml) water

1 Blend or process ingredients until smooth.
nutritional count per serving 0.2g total fat (0g saturated fat); 163kJ (39 cal); 7.7g carbohydrate; 1.7g protein; 3.6g fibre
tip For something refreshing, freeze the juice until almost set then scrape with a fork for a granita-like snack.

juices

left peach, apple and strawberry **centre** watercress, beetroot and celery **right** strawberry and papaya

left orange and ginger **centre** raspberry and peach **right** mixed berry

orange and ginger

3 medium oranges (720g)
2cm piece fresh ginger (10g), grated

1 Juice oranges on citrus squeezer; pour into glass.
2 Stir in ginger.
nutritional count per serving 0.6g total fat
(0g saturated fat); 807kJ (193 cal); 40.9g carbohydrate;
5.2g protein; 10.5g fibre

mixed berry

3 strawberries (60g)
¼ cup (40g) blueberries
¼ cup (35g) raspberries
⅓ cup (80ml) water

1 Blend or process ingredients until smooth;
pour into glass.
nutritional count per serving 0.2g total fat
(0g saturated fat); 184kJ (44 cal); 8.2g carbohydrate;
1.7g protein; 3.9g fibre
tip For something refreshing, freeze the juice until
almost set then scrape with a fork for a granita-
like snack.

raspberry and peach

1 large peach (220g), chopped coarsely
¼ cup (35g) raspberries
½ cup (125ml) water

1 Blend or process peach and raspberry until smooth;
pour into glass.
2 Stir in the water.
nutritional count per serving 0.3g total fat
(0g saturated fat); 301kJ (72 cal); 14.1g carbohydrate;
2.1g protein; 4.5g fibre

watermelon and mint

450g watermelon
4 fresh mint leaves

1 Blend or process ingredients until smooth; pour into glass.
nutritional count per serving 0.6g total fat (0g saturated fat); 280kJ (67 cal); 14.5g carbohydrate; 0.9g protein; 1.9g fibre

pineapple, orange and strawberry

1 small orange (180g), peeled, quartered
150g pineapple, chopped coarsely
2 strawberries (40g)
¼ cup (60ml) water

1 Push orange, pineapple and strawberries through juice extractor into glass; stir in the water.
nutritional count per serving 0.3g total fat (0g saturated fat); 468kJ (112 cal); 23.2g carbohydrate; 3.5g protein; 6.6g fibre

beetroot, carrot and spinach

1 small beetroot (100g), cut into wedges
1 small carrot (70g), chopped coarsely
20g baby spinach leaves
½ cup (125ml) water

1 Push beetroot, carrot and spinach through juice extractor into glass.
2 Stir in the water.
nutritional count per serving 0.2g total fat (0g saturated fat); 238kJ (57 cal); 11.2g carbohydrate; 2.7g protein; 5.3g fibre

left watermelon and mint **centre** pineapple, orange and strawberry **right** beetroot, carrot and spinach

left strawberry, honey and soy smoothie **centre** apple and pear **right** silver beet, apple and celery

strawberry, honey and soy smoothie

6 strawberries (120g)
½ cup (125ml) soy milk
1 teaspoon honey

1 Blend or process ingredients until smooth; pour into glass.
nutritional count per serving 3.6g total fat (0.4g saturated fat); 472kJ (113 cal); 14.4g carbohydrate; 6.2g protein; 3.2g fibre

silver beet, apple and celery

We used a green apple in this recipe, but you can use the colour of your choice.

1 trimmed silver beet leaf (80g), chopped coarsely
1 large apple (200g), cut into wedges
1 trimmed celery stalk (100g), chopped coarsely

1 Push ingredients through juice extractor into glass; stir to combine.
nutritional count per serving 0.5g total fat (0g saturated fat); 460kJ (110 cal); 24.6g carbohydrate; 2.4g protein; 7.8g fibre

apple and pear

We used a green apple in this recipe, but you can use the colour of your choice.

1 medium apple (150g), cut into wedges
1 medium pear (230g), cut into wedges

1 Push ingredients through juice extractor into glass; stir to combine.
nutritional count per serving 0.4g total fat (0g saturated fat); 853kJ (204 cal); 51.3g carbohydrate; 1.1g protein; 9g fibre

mango and grapefruit

1 small grapefruit (350g)
1 small mango (300g), chopped coarsely
¼ cup (60ml) water

1 Juice grapefruit on citrus squeezer; pour into glass.
2 Blend or process mango and the water until smooth. Transfer to same glass; stir to combine.
nutritional count per serving 0.9g total fat
(0g saturated fat); 757kJ (181 cal); 37.8g carbohydrate;
4.2g protein; 4.6g fibre

apple and celery

We used green apples in this recipe, but you can use the colour of your choice.

2 small apples (260g), cut into wedges
1 trimmed celery stalk (100g), chopped coarsely

1 Push ingredients through juice extractor into glass; stir to combine.
nutritional count per serving 0.4g total fat
(0g saturated fat); 598kJ (143 cal); 34.7g carbohydrate;
1.4g protein; 7g fibre

pear and grape

1 medium pear (230g), cut into wedges
175g seedless red grapes

1 Push ingredients through juice extractor into glass; stir to combine.
nutritional count per serving 0.4g total fat
(0g saturated fat); 953kJ (228 cal); 55.6g carbohydrate;
2.8g protein; 7.3g fibre

left mango and grapefruit **centre** apple and celery **right** pear and grape

left pineapple, ginger and mint **centre** ginger, orange and pineapple **right** mandarin

pineapple, ginger and mint

You need ½ small pineapple for this recipe.

400g pineapple, chopped coarsely
1 cup firmly packed fresh mint leaves
1cm piece fresh ginger (5g)

1 Push ingredients through juice extractor into glass; stir to combine.
nutritional count per serving 0.8g total fat (0.1g saturated fat); 418kJ (100 cal); 19.1g carbohydrate; 3.7g protein; 8.1g fibre

mandarin

3 small mandarins (300g)

1 Juice mandarins on citrus squeezer; pour into glass.
nutritional count per serving 0.4g total fat (0g saturated fat); 343kJ (82 cal); 17g carbohydrate; 1.9g protein; 4.3g fibre

ginger, orange and pineapple

You need ¼ small pineapple for this recipe.

1 medium orange (240g)
200g pineapple, chopped coarsely
2cm piece fresh ginger (10g)

1 Juice orange on citrus squeezer; pour into glass.
2 Blend or process pineapple and ginger until smooth. Stir into orange juice.
nutritional count per serving 0.3g total fat (0g saturated fat); 22.2g carbohydrate; 439kJ (105 cal); 2.8g protein; 5.9g fibre

tangelo and ginger

2 medium tangelos (420g)
2cm piece fresh ginger (10g), grated

1   Juice tangelos on citrus squeezer; pour into glass.
2   Stir in ginger.
nutritional count per serving 0.3g total fat
(0g saturated fat); 477kJ (114 cal); 23.7g carbohydrate;
1.9g protein; 6.2g fibre

kiwi fruit and green grape

3 medium kiwi fruits (255g), quartered
70g seedless green grapes
¼ cup (60ml) water

1   Blend or process ingredients until smooth;
pour into glass.
nutritional count per serving 0.5g total fat
(0g saturated fat); 623kJ (149 cal); 31.8g carbohydrate;
3.5g protein; 7.8g fibre

grapefruit and blood orange

2 small blood oranges (360g)
1 small grapefruit (350g)

1   Juice oranges and grapefruit on citrus squeezer;
pour into glass.
nutritional count per serving 0.7g total fat
(0g saturated fat); 652kJ (156 cal); 31.2g carbohydrate;
4.6g protein; 6.5g fibre

left tangelo and ginger **centre** kiwi fruit and green grape **right** grapefruit and blood orange

left pear and ginger **centre** orange, mango and strawberry **right** orange, carrot and celery

pear and ginger

2 medium pears (460g), cut into wedges
2cm piece fresh ginger (10g)

1 Push ingredients through juice extractor into glass; stir to combine.
nutritional count per serving 0.5g total fat (0g saturated fat); 882kJ (211 cal); 52.6g carbohydrate; 1.3g protein; 9.8g fibre

orange, carrot and celery

1 large orange (300g), peeled, quartered
1 large carrot (180g), chopped coarsely
1 trimmed celery stalk (100g), chopped coarsely

1 Push orange, carrot and celery through juice extractor into glass; stir to combine.
nutritional count per serving 0.5g total fat (0g saturated fat); 573kJ (137 cal); 28.6g carbohydrate; 4.2g protein; 11.3g fibre

orange, mango and strawberry

2 small oranges (360g)
1 small mango (300g), chopped coarsely
3 strawberries (60g), chopped coarsely

1 Juice oranges on citrus squeezer; pour into glass.
2 Blend or process mango and strawberries until smooth; stir into orange juice.
nutritional count per serving 0.7g total fat (0g saturated fat); 949kJ (227 cal); 48.7g carbohydrate; 5.7g protein; 9.6g fibre

banana
soy smoothie

1 cup (250ml) soy milk
1 small banana (130g), chopped coarsely

1 Blend or process ingredients until smooth;
pour into glass.
nutritional count per serving 2.1g total fat
(0.2g saturated fat); 255kJ (61 cal); 8.2g carbohydrate;
8.2g protein; 0.9g fibre

carrot, ginger
and silver beet

2 medium carrots (240g), chopped coarsely
3 trimmed silver beet leaves (240g), chopped coarsely
2cm piece fresh ginger (10g)

1 Push ingredients through juice extractor into glass;
stir to combine.
nutritional count per serving 0.7g total fat
(0g saturated fat); 364kJ (87 cal); 14.5g carbohydrate;
5.4g protein; 13.1g fibre

orange, carrot
and ginger

2 medium oranges (480g), peeled, quartered
1 small carrot (70g), chopped coarsely
2cm piece fresh ginger (10g)

1 Push orange, carrot and ginger through juice
extractor into glass; stir to combine.
nutritional count per serving 0.4g total fat
(0g saturated fat); 606kJ (145 cal); 30.6g carbohydrate;
4g protein; 8.8g fibre

left banana soy smoothie **centre** carrot, ginger and silver beet **right** orange, carrot and ginger

vegetable stock

2 medium brown onions (300g),
   chopped coarsely
3 medium carrots (360g),
   chopped coarsely
3 medium parsnips (750g),
   chopped coarsely
2 medium swedes (450g),
   chopped coarsely
1 small fennel bulb (200g),
   chopped coarsely
1 large red capsicum (350g),
   chopped coarsely
1 trimmed celery stalk (100g),
   chopped coarsely
2 cloves garlic, chopped coarsely
2 bay leaves
6 black peppercorns
4 litres (16 cups) water
1¼ cups coarsely chopped fresh
   flat-leaf parsley

1   Combine vegetables, bay leaves, peppercorns and the water in large stock pot or saucepan; bring to the boil. Reduce heat; simmer, uncovered, stirring occasionally, 1 hour. Add parsley; simmer, uncovered, 30 minutes.
2   Strain stock through muslin-lined sieve or colander; discard solids.
preparation time 30 minutes **cooking time 1** hour 40 minutes
makes 2 litres
nutritional count per 250ml 0.4g total fat (0g saturated fat); 343kJ (82 cal); 15.8g carbohydrate; 3.8g protein; 6.5g fibre
tip Stock can be kept, covered, for up to a week in the refrigerator. Stock also suitable to freeze for up to three months

soups

asian broth

roasted tomato and capsicum soup

asian broth

5 dried shiitake mushrooms (10g)
1½ cups (375ml) vegetable stock (page 60)
2 teaspoons tamari
1cm piece fresh ginger (5g), grated
½ teaspoon peanut oil
½ small carrot (35g), sliced thinly
30g snow peas, trimmed,
  chopped coarsely
1 green onion, sliced thinly
½ cup (40g) finely shredded wombok
30g canned bamboo shoots,
  cut into matchsticks

1 Place mushrooms in small heatproof bowl, cover with boiling water, stand 20 minutes; drain. Discard stems; halve caps.
2 Combine stock, tamari, ginger and oil in medium saucepan; bring to the boil. Add mushroom and carrot, reduce heat; simmer, covered, until carrot is just tender. Add peas, onion, wombok and bamboo shoots; simmer, uncovered, 2 minutes.
preparation time 15 minutes (plus standing time)
cooking time 10 minutes **serves** 1
nutritional count per serving 2.6g total fat (0.4g saturated fat); 410kJ (98 cal); 13.8g carbohydrate; 4.6g protein; 6.6g fibre

roasted tomato and capsicum soup

4 large tomatoes (880g),
  chopped coarsely
1 large red capsicum (350g),
  chopped coarsely
1 small brown onion (80g),
  chopped coarsely
2 cloves garlic, sliced thinly
1 tablespoon finely shredded fresh basil

1 Preheat oven to 180°C/160°C fan-forced.
2 Combine tomato, capsicum, onion and garlic in small baking dish; roast, covered, about 30 minutes or until vegetables soften.
3 Push vegetables through mouli or fine sieve into small saucepan; discard solids.
4 Reheat soup; serve soup topped with basil.
preparation time 10 minutes **cooking time** 35 minutes **serves** 1
nutritional count per serving 1.6g total fat (0g saturated fat); 895kJ (214 cal); 33.1g carbohydrate; 14.9g protein; 15.4g fibre

vegetable soup

2 cups (500ml) vegetable stock (page 60)
1 trimmed corn cob (250g)
½ cup (50g) coarsely chopped cauliflower
½ small carrot (35g), diced into
   1cm pieces
30g snow peas, trimmed, sliced thinly
1 green onion, sliced thinly

1 Bring stock to the boil in small saucepan. Cut kernels from corn cob, add to pan with cauliflower and carrot; return to the boil. Reduce heat; simmer, covered, about 10 minutes or until cauliflower is just tender.
2 Stir in snow peas and onion; simmer, uncovered, 2 minutes.
preparation time 10 minutes **cooking time** 20 minutes **serves** 1
nutritional count per serving 2.7g total fat (0.2g saturated fat); 1074kJ (257 cal); 45g carbohydrate; 12.6g protein; 15.3g fibre

leek and potato soup

1 teaspoon olive oil
1 clove garlic, crushed
½ teaspoon fresh thyme leaves
1 small leek (200g), sliced thinly
1 medium potato (200g),
   chopped coarsely
2 cups (500ml) vegetable stock (page 60)
½ green onion, sliced thinly

1 Heat oil in small saucepan; cook garlic, thyme and leek, stirring, about 3 minutes or until leek softens. Add potato and stock; bring to the boil. Reduce heat; simmer, covered, about 15 minutes or until potato is tender.
2 Blend or process leek mixture until smooth.
3 Reheat soup; serve soup topped with onion.
preparation time 10 minutes **cooking time** 25 minutes **serves** 1
nutritional count per serving 5.5g total fat (0.7g saturated fat); 1016kJ (243 cal); 38.5g carbohydrate; 9.3g protein; 11.1g fibre

vegetable soup

leek and potato soup

pumpkin and kumara soup

vegetable and soba soup

pumpkin and kumara soup

1 teaspoon olive oil
1 small brown onion (80g),
  chopped coarsely
1 clove garlic, crushed
200g pumpkin, chopped coarsely
1 small kumara (250g), chopped coarsely
2 cups (500ml) vegetable stock (page 60)
¼ teaspoon finely grated orange rind
1 tablespoon fresh orange juice
1 tablespoon finely chopped
  fresh chives

1 Heat oil in medium saucepan; cook onion and garlic, stirring, until onion softens.
2 Add pumpkin, kumara and stock; bring to the boil. Reduce heat; simmer, covered, about 15 minutes or until pumpkin and kumara are tender. Cool 10 minutes.
3 Blend or process pumpkin mixture until smooth.
4 Return soup mixture to same pan with rind and juice; stir over heat, without boiling, until heated through.
5 Serve soup topped with chives.

preparation time 15 minutes **cooking time** 25 minutes **serves** 1
nutritional count per serving 6g total fat (1.3g saturated fat); 1438kJ (344 cal); 60.1g carbohydrate; 12.2g protein; 12.2g fibre

vegetable and soba soup

2 cups (500ml) vegetable stock (page 60)
1 teaspoon tamari
5cm piece fresh ginger (25g), grated
2 cloves garlic, crushed
1 small carrot (70g), cut into matchsticks
50g snow peas, trimmed,
  sliced thinly lengthways
50g soba noodles

1 Combine stock, tamari, ginger and garlic in small saucepan; bring to the boil. Reduce heat; simmer, covered, 5 minutes. Add carrot and snow peas; simmer, uncovered, about 3 minutes or until carrot is tender.
2 Meanwhile, cook noodles in small saucepan of boiling water, uncovered, until just tender; drain.
3 Place noodles in serving bowl; ladle soup over noodles.

preparation time 15 minutes **cooking time** 15 minutes **serves** 1
nutritional count per serving 1.2g total fat (0.2g saturated fat); 1108kJ (265 cal); 51.8g carbohydrate; 10.9g protein; 10.5g fibre
tip Soba is a Japanese noodle, similar in appearance to spaghetti, made from buckwheat.

lentil and vegetable soup

French green lentils have a sensational nutty, earthy flavour and stand up well to being boiled without becoming muddy. They are available at specialist food shops and better delicatessens. You need the leaves from the celery stalk for this recipe.

2 cups (500ml) vegetable stock (page 60)
¼ cup (50g) french green lentils
1 clove garlic, crushed
½ untrimmed celery stalk (75g)
1 medium carrot (120g),
    chopped coarsely
50g mushrooms, chopped coarsely
2 tablespoons coarsely chopped
    fresh flat-leaf parsley

1   Combine stock, lentils, garlic and celery leaves in small saucepan; bring to the boil. Reduce heat; simmer, covered, about 20 minutes or until lentils just soften. Discard celery leaves.
2   Add coarsely chopped celery stalk, carrot and mushroom; bring to the boil. Reduce heat; simmer, covered, about 15 minutes or until vegetables are tender. Stir in parsley.

preparation time 10 minutes cooking time 45 minutes serves 1
nutritional count per serving 1.7g total fat (0.2g saturated fat); 978kJ (234 cal); 37.5g carbohydrate; 18g protein; 17.7g fibre

stir-fried asian greens with tofu

2 teaspoons peanut oil
2cm piece fresh ginger (10g),
   cut into slivers
1 clove garlic, crushed
100g gai lan, chopped coarsely
100g broccolini, chopped coarsely
150g baby buk choy, chopped coarsely
100g firm tofu, chopped coarsely
1 tablespoon water
2 teaspoons tamari
2 teaspoons coarsely chopped
   roasted peanuts

1 Heat oil in wok; stir-fry ginger and garlic until fragrant. Add vegetables, tofu, the water and tamari; stir-fry until greens are just tender.
2 Serve stir-fry sprinkled with nuts.

preparation time 10 minutes **cooking time** 10 minutes **serves** 1 **nutritional count per serving** 19.6g total fat (3.1g saturated fat); 1221kJ (292 cal); 6.1g carbohydrate; 23g protein; 12.8g fibre

vegetable dishes

roasted cherry tomatoes, broccolini and pepitas

ratatouille

roasted cherry tomatoes, broccolini and pepitas

1 teaspoon olive oil
1 small red onion (100g), sliced thinly
2 cloves garlic, crushed
125g cherry tomatoes, halved
1 tablespoon cider vinegar
250g broccolini
2 tablespoons toasted pepitas

1 Preheat oven to 200°C/180°C fan-forced.
2 Combine oil and onion in small baking dish; roast, uncovered, 10 minutes. Add garlic, tomato and vinegar; roast, uncovered, about 10 minutes or until tomato softens.
3 Meanwhile, boil, steam or microwave broccolini until tender; drain.
4 Serve brocollini topped with tomato mixture and seeds.
preparation time 10 minutes cooking time 20 minutes serves 1
nutritional count per serving 16.7g total fat (0.7g saturated fat); 1379kJ (330 cal); 10.3g carbohydrate; 14.2g protein; 17.9g fibre

ratatouille

1 small red capsicum (150g)
1 small yellow capsicum (150g)
1 teaspoon olive oil
1 clove garlic, crushed
½ small red onion (50g), chopped coarsely
1 baby eggplant (60g), sliced thickly
1 small zucchini (90g), sliced thickly
2 large tomatoes (440g), peeled, chopped coarsely
100g mushrooms, sliced thickly
1 tablespoon fresh lemon juice
1 tablespoon coarsely chopped fresh flat-leaf parsley

1 Quarter capsicums; discard seeds and membranes. Roast under grill or in very hot oven, skin-side up, until skin blisters and blackens. Cover capsicum pieces with plastic or paper for 5 minutes; peel away skin then chop capsicum coarsely.
2 Meanwhile, heat oil in medium saucepan; cook garlic, onion, eggplant, zucchini, tomato and mushroom, covered, over medium heat, stirring occasionally, 10 minutes. Stir in capsicum; cook, uncovered, until heated through. Stir in juice and parsley.
preparation time 20 minutes cooking time 25 minutes serves 1
nutritional count per serving 6.2g total fat (0.7g saturated fat); 895kJ (214 cal); 23.9g carbohydrate; 14.3g protein; 13.9g fibre

vegetable dishes

roasted vegetable stack

1 baby fennel bulb (130g)
1 medium egg tomato (75g),
   halved lengthways
½ small red capsicum (75g), sliced thickly
½ medium zucchini (60g),
   sliced thickly lengthways
1 baby eggplant (60g), sliced thickly
cooking-oil spray
1 tablespoon finely chopped fresh
   flat-leaf parsley
1 tablespoon fresh lemon juice
1 teaspoon olive oil

1 Preheat oven to 200°C/180°C fan-forced.
2 Reserve fennel tips from fennel; slice fennel thinly.
3 Place vegetables on lightly oiled oven tray; spray with oil. Roast, uncovered, about 20 minutes or until vegetables soften. Stir in half of the parsley.
4 Stack vegetables on serving plate; drizzle with combined juice and oil, sprinkle with remaining parsley and coarsely chopped reserved fennel tips.

preparation time 10 minutes cooking time 20 minutes serves 1
nutritional count per serving 7.2g total fat (0.8g saturated fat); 514kJ (123 cal); 9.7g carbohydrate; 4.1g protein; 6.5g fibre

black-eyed beans with kumara, shallots and garlic

⅓ cup (65g) dried black-eyed beans
1 teaspoon olive oil
5 shallots (125g)
5 cloves garlic, unpeeled
1 small kumara (250g), chopped coarsely
2 tablespoons fresh lemon juice
1 small radicchio, shredded finely
1 tablespoon finely chopped fresh
   flat-leaf parsley

1 Place beans in small bowl, cover with water; stand overnight, drain. Rinse under cold water; drain.
2 Preheat oven to 200°C/180°C fan-forced.
3 Combine oil, shallots, garlic and kumara on oven tray. Roast, uncovered, about 20 minutes or until garlic softens. Remove garlic from tray. Return remaining vegetables to oven; roast, uncovered, about 15 minutes or until vegetables are browned lightly.
4 Meanwhile, place beans in small saucepan of boiling water; bring to the boil. Reduce heat; simmer, covered, about 25 minutes or until beans are tender. Drain.
5 Using fingers, squeeze garlic from skins into medium bowl; stir in juice.
6 Add beans, vegetables, radicchio and parsley; toss gently to combine.

preparation time 20 minutes (plus standing time)
cooking time 35 minutes serves 1
nutritional count per serving 6.1g total fat (0.8g saturated fat); 1078kJ (258 cal); 39.1g carbohydrate; 10.3g protein; 12.1g fibre

roasted vegetable stack

black-eyed beans with kumara, shallots and garlic

dhal with vegetables

brown rice with vegetables and tahini dressing

dhal with vegetables

1 teaspoon vegetable oil
2cm piece fresh ginger (10g), grated
4cm piece fresh turmeric (20g), grated
1 clove garlic, crushed
½ cup (100g) yellow split peas
1 small carrot (70g), chopped coarsely
2 cups (500ml) water
1 small zucchini (90g), chopped coarsely
ginger yogurt
1 tablespoon finely chopped
   fresh coriander
1cm piece fresh ginger (5g), grated
1 tablespoon fresh lime juice
2 tablespoons sheep milk yogurt

1 Heat oil in medium saucepan; cook ginger, turmeric and garlic, stirring, until fragrant. Add peas, carrot and the water; bring to the boil. Reduce heat; simmer, covered, about 25 minutes or until peas are almost tender. Add zucchini; cook, covered, about 5 minutes or until zucchini is just tender.
2 Meanwhile, combine ingredients for ginger yogurt in small bowl.
3 Serve dhal with ginger yogurt.

preparation time 10 minutes **cooking time** 35 minutes **serves** 1
nutritional count per serving 10g total fat (0.8g saturated fat); 1764kJ (422 cal); 54.8g carbohydrate; 27.3g protein; 14.5g fibre

brown rice with vegetables and tahini dressing

¼ cup (50g) brown long-grain rice
1 small zucchini (90g), sliced thinly
2 medium yellow patty-pan squash
   (60g), quartered
1 small carrot (70g), grated coarsely
¼ cup finely chopped fresh
   flat-leaf parsley
1 tablespoon sunflower seeds
tahini dressing
1 tablespoon tahini
2 teaspoons fresh lemon juice
1 tablespoon water
1 clove garlic, crushed

1 Cook rice in small saucepan of boiling water, uncovered, until rice is tender; drain.
2 Meanwhile, boil, steam or microwave zucchini and squash, separately, until tender; drain.
3 Combine rice in small bowl with carrot, parsley and seeds.
4 Place ingredients for tahini dressing in screw-top jar; shake well.
5 Serve rice and vegetables drizzled with dressing.

preparation time 15 minutes **cooking time** 20 minutes **serves** 1
nutritional count per serving 24.4g total fat (2.7g saturated fat); 1965kJ (470 cal); 46.6g carbohydrate; 16g protein; 12.6g fibre

baked potato with guacamole

1 medium potato (200g)
1 small avocado (200g)
½ small red onion (50g), chopped finely
1 small tomato (90g), seeded,
  chopped finely
1 tablespoon finely chopped
  fresh coriander
1 tablespoon fresh lime juice
50g mesclun

1 Preheat oven to 200°C/180°C fan-forced.

2 Pierce potato skin in several places with fork, wrap potato in foil; place on oven tray. Bake about 1 hour or until tender.

3 Mash avocado coarsely in small bowl; stir in onion, tomato, coriander and juice.

4 Cut a deep cross in potato; serve potato topped with guacamole accompanied with mesclun.

preparation time 15 minutes cooking time 1 hour serves 1
nutritional count per serving 32g total fat (6.9g saturated fat); 1818kJ (435 cal); 27.4g carbohydrate; 8.6g protein; 7.1g fibre

leek, goat cheese and brown lentil bake

⅓ cup (65g) brown lentils
1 bay leaf
1 medium leek (350g), sliced thinly
2 tablespoons fresh lemon juice
2 cloves garlic, crushed
¼ cup (60ml) vegetable stock (page 60)
40g goat cheese, crumbled
1 tablespoon coarsely chopped
  fresh chives

1 Preheat oven to 180°C/160°C fan-forced.

2 Combine lentils and bay leaf in small saucepan, cover with water; bring to the boil. Reduce heat; simmer, covered, about 10 minutes or until lentils are almost tender. Drain; discard bay leaf.

3 Combine lentils, leek, juice, garlic and stock in 3-cup (750ml) ovenproof dish. Bake, covered, about 40 minutes or until the leek is tender, stirring halfway through cooking.

4 Preheat grill.

5 Sprinkle lentil mixture with cheese; place under grill 3 minutes or until cheese browns lightly. Sprinkle with chives.

preparation time 15 minutes cooking time 1 hour serves 1
nutritional count per serving 7.6g total fat (4.2g saturated fat); 819kJ (196 cal); 18.1g carbohydrate; 13.2g protein; 9.8g fibre

baked potato with guacamole

leek, goat cheese and brown lentil bake

roasted root vegetables with yogurt

eggplant with salsa fresca

roasted root vegetables with yogurt

1 small parsnip (120g), chopped coarsely

100g celeriac, chopped coarsely

150g pumpkin, chopped coarsely

1 medium potato (200g),
chopped coarsely

2 cloves garlic, crushed

1 teaspoon finely chopped
fresh rosemary

2 teaspoons olive oil

½ small red capsicum (75g),
chopped finely

1 tablespoon coarsely chopped
fresh chives

2 tablespoons goat milk yogurt

1   Preheat oven to 200°C/180°C fan-forced.

2   Combine parsnip, celeriac, pumpkin, potato, garlic, rosemary and oil on oven tray. Roast, uncovered, about 35 minutes or until vegetables are tender. Add capsicum and chives; toss gently to combine.

3   Serve vegetables topped with yogurt and lemon wedges, if desired.

preparation time 15 minutes cooking time 35 minutes   serves 1
nutritional count per serving 12.2g total fat (2.8g saturated fat);
1542kJ (369 cal); 51.3g carbohydrate; 13.2g protein; 12.3g fibre

eggplant with salsa fresca

3 baby eggplants (180g),
halved lengthways

salsa fresca

½ small green capsicum (75g),
chopped finely

½ small yellow capsicum (75g),
chopped finely

1 small tomato (90g), seeded,
chopped finely

2 tablespoons finely shredded
fresh basil

2 tablespoons fresh lemon juice

1   Cook eggplant on heated oiled grill plate (or grill or barbecue) until tender.

2   Combine ingredients for salsa fresca in small bowl.

3   Serve grilled eggplant topped with salsa fresca.

preparation time 15 minutes cooking time 15 minutes serves 1
nutritional count per serving 0.8g total fat (0g saturated fat);
288kJ (69 cal); 9.6g carbohydrate; 4.6g protein; 5.9g fibre

stir-fried asian greens with mixed mushrooms

2 teaspoons sesame oil
1 clove garlic, crushed
10cm stick fresh lemon grass (20g),
    chopped finely
2cm piece fresh ginger (10g), grated
150g oyster mushrooms,
    chopped coarsely
150g button mushrooms,
    chopped coarsely
150g baby buk choy, chopped coarsely
¼ small wombok (175g),
    chopped coarsely

1 Heat oil in wok; stir-fry garlic, lemon grass, ginger and mushrooms until browned lightly. Add bok choy and cabbage; stir-fry until greens are just wilted.
2 Serve stir-fry with lime wedges, if desired.
preparation time 10 minutes cooking time 5 minutes serves 1
nutritional count per serving 10.7g total fat (1.3g saturated fat); 757kJ (181 cal); 7.4g carbohydrate; 13.9g protein; 15.2g fibre

chickpea patties with tomato and cucumber salad

1 medium potato (200g)
300g can chickpeas, drained, rinsed
1 clove garlic, crushed
1 green onion, sliced thinly
⅓ cup coarsely chopped fresh coriander
1 tablespoon polenta
1 lebanese cucumber (130g)
1 small egg tomato (60g), sliced thickly
1 tablespoon fresh lime juice
1 teaspoon pepitas
1 teaspoon sesame seeds
¼ cup (70g) sheep milk yogurt

1 Boil, steam or microwave potato until tender; drain. Mash potato and chickpeas in medium bowl; stir in garlic, onion and coriander. Using hands; shape mixture into two patties. Coat with polenta; refrigerate 1 hour.
2 Preheat oven to 180°C/160°C fan-forced.
3 Cook patties in oiled medium frying pan until browned lightly. Transfer to oven tray; bake about 15 minutes or until patties are heated through.
4 Meanwhile, slice half of the cucumber thinly; combine in medium bowl with tomato, juice and seeds. Cut remaining cucumber coarsely; combine in small bowl with yogurt.
5 Serve patties with salad and yogurt.
preparation time 20 minutes (plus refrigeration time)
cooking time 40 minutes serves 1
nutritional count per serving 21.1g total fat (1.4g saturated fat); 2491kJ (596 cal); 64.6g carbohydrate; 24.5g protein; 18.5g fibre

stir-fried asian greens with mixed mushrooms

chickpea patties with tomato and cucumber salad

stir-fried tofu with vegetables and lemon grass

brown rice pilaf

stir-fried tofu with vegetables and lemon grass

1 teaspoon sesame oil
100g firm tofu, diced into 1cm pieces
1 small red capsicum (150g), sliced thinly
300g baby buk choy, chopped coarsely
10cm stick fresh lemon grass (20g),
    chopped finely
1 clove garlic, crushed
¼ cup loosely packed fresh
    coriander leaves

1 Heat oil in wok; stir-fry tofu, capsicum, buk choy, lemon grass and garlic until vegetables are just tender. Stir in coriander.
2 Serve stir-fry with lemon wedges, if desired.
preparation time 10 minutes cooking time 5 minutes serves 1
nutritional count per serving 12.4g total fat (1.7g saturated fat); 924kJ (221 cal); 9.7g carbohydrate; 17.7g protein; 8.2g fibre

brown rice pilaf

1 small kumara (250g), chopped coarsely
cooking-oil spray
1½ cups (375ml) vegetable stock (page 60)
1 teaspoon olive oil
1 small brown onion (80g),
    chopped finely
1 clove garlic, crushed
1 trimmed celery stalk (100g),
    chopped finely
70g mushrooms, chopped coarsely
¾ cup (150g) brown medium-grain rice
1 tablespoon finely grated lemon rind
¼ cup loosely packed fresh flat-leaf
    parsley leaves

1 Preheat oven to 180°C/160°C fan-forced.
2 Place kumara on lightly oiled oven tray; spray with oil. Roast, uncovered, about 25 minutes or until tender.
3 Meanwhile, bring stock to the boil in small saucepan. Reduce heat; simmer, uncovered.
4 Heat oil in medium saucepan; cook onion, garlic and celery, stirring, until onion softens. Add mushroom and rice; cook, stirring, 2 minutes. Add stock, reduce heat; simmer, covered, about 50 minutes or until stock is absorbed and rice is tender. Stir in kumara, rind and parsley.
preparation time 15 minutes cooking time 1 hour serves 1
nutritional count per serving 11.1g total fat (1.6g saturated fat); 3515kJ (841 cal); 161.4g carbohydrate; 22.2g protein; 18g fibre

These dips are best served with assorted crudités such as carrot, cucumber and capsicum sticks. Each dip serves 1.

hummus

1½ cups (375ml) water
300g can chickpeas, drained, rinsed
2 tablespoons fresh lemon juice
1 clove garlic, quartered

1 Place the water and chickpeas in small saucepan; bring to the boil. Boil, uncovered, 10 minutes. Strain chickpeas over small bowl; reserve ⅓ cup cooking liquid. Cool 10 minutes.
2 Blend or process chickpeas, juice and garlic with reserved cooking liquid until just smooth.
3 Serve hummus sprinkled with finely chopped fresh flat-leaf parsley, if desired.
preparation time 5 minutes **cooking time** 15 minutes
nutritional count per serving 4.3g total fat
(0.6g saturated fat); 861kJ (206 cal); 28.5g carbohydrate; 13g protein; 9.9g fibre

carrot dip

1 medium carrot (120g), grated coarsely
½ cup (125ml) fresh orange juice
2 tablespoons goat milk yogurt
1 tablespoon finely chopped fresh mint
1 tablespoon dried currants
1cm piece fresh ginger (5g), grated

1 Place carrot and juice in small saucepan; cook, uncovered, over low heat, about 10 minutes or until liquid is evaporated. Cool 10 minutes.
2 Blend or process carrot mixture with yogurt; stir in mint, currants and ginger.
preparation time 10 minutes **cooking time** 10 minutes
nutritional count per serving 2.2g total fat
(1.2g saturated fat); 569kJ (136 cal); 26g carbohydrate; 3.8g protein; 4.4g fibre

raita

½ cup (140g) sheep milk yogurt
½ lebanese cucumber (65g), chopped finely
1 tablespoon finely chopped fresh coriander
1 clove garlic, crushed
2 teaspoons fresh lemon juice

1 Combine ingredients in small bowl.
preparation time 10 minutes
nutritional count per serving 3.8g total fat
(0g saturated fat); 293kJ (70 cal); 3.9g carbohydrate;
3.2g protein; 0.7g fibre

beetroot dip

225g can beetroot slices, drained
¼ cup (70g) sheep milk yogurt

1 Blend or process beetroot with yogurt.
2 Serve beetroot dip sprinkled with coarsely chopped
chives, if desired.
preparation time 5 minutes
nutritional count per serving 4.4g total fat
(0g saturated fat); 569kJ (136 cal); 17.6g carbohydrate;
5.3g protein; 4g fibre

green vegetable salad with american mustard dressing

50g green beans, trimmed
50g snow peas, trimmed
50g sugar snap peas, trimmed
¼ cup loosely packed fresh
   flat-leaf parsley leaves
2 tablespoons fresh chervil leaves
1 cup (25g) baby rocket leaves
1 tablespoon dried currants
american mustard dressing
2 teaspoons american mustard
2 teaspoons fresh lemon juice
2 teaspoons olive oil

1 Boil, steam or microwave beans and peas, separately, until just tender; drain. Rinse beans and peas under cold water; drain.
2 Meanwhile, place ingredients for american mustard dressing in screw-top jar; shake well.
3 Place beans and peas in medium bowl with herbs, rocket and currants; toss gently to combine.
4 Serve salad drizzled with dressing.
preparation time 10 minutes **cooking time** 10 minutes **serves** 1
nutritional count per serving 9.9g total fat (1.3g saturated fat); 715kJ (171 cal); 15g carbohydrate; 5.7g protein; 5.6g fibre

big salads

lamb's lettuce salad with pecans and orange

orange, fennel and almond salad

lamb's lettuce salad with pecans and orange

20g watercress
25g lamb's lettuce
30g snow pea sprouts, trimmed
⅓ cup (45g) toasted pecans,
    chopped coarsely
2 teaspoons olive oil
2 small oranges (360g)

1 Place watercress, lettuce, sprouts, nuts and oil in medium bowl.
2 Segment oranges over salad to save juice. Add orange segments to bowl; toss gently to combine.
preparation time 10 minutes **serves** 1
nutritional count per serving 42.1g total fat (3.4g saturated fat); 2241kJ (536 cal); 29.8g carbohydrate; 10.6g protein; 11.6g fibre
tip Lamb's lettuce, also known as mâche or corn salad, has a mild, almost nutty, flavour and tender, narrow, dark green leaves. You need a 225g punnet for this recipe. It is available from most greengrocers.

orange, fennel and almond salad

⅓ cup (80ml) fresh orange juice
2 teaspoons almond oil
1 baby fennel bulb (130g)
1 large orange (300g), segmented
50g baby spinach leaves
¼ cup (20g) flaked almonds

1 Place juice in small saucepan; bring to the boil. Boil, uncovered, until juice reduces to 1 tablespoon; cool 10 minutes. Combine juice and oil in small jug.
2 Meanwhile, reserve fennel tips from fennel; slice fennel thinly.
3 Place fennel in medium bowl with orange, spinach and nuts; toss gently to combine.
4 Serve salad drizzled with dressing and sprinkled with fennel tips.
preparation time 10 minutes **cooking time** 10 minutes **serves** 1
nutritional count per serving 20.8g total fat (1.5g saturated fat); 1363kJ (326 cal); 26.5g carbohydrate; 8.5g protein; 9.6g fibre

greek salad

½ baby cos lettuce (90g), leaves
  separated
1 medium tomato (150g),
  cut into thick wedges
½ small red capsicum (75g),
  chopped coarsely
1 lebanese cucumber (130g),
  chopped coarsely
¼ cup (40g) seeded kalamata olives
50g goat milk fetta cheese, crumbled
2 teaspoons fresh lemon juice
2 teaspoons olive oil

1   Place ingredients in large bowl; toss gently to combine.
preparation time 10 minutes **serves** 1
nutritional count per serving 18.1g total fat (6.6g saturated fat);
1196kJ (286 cal); 19.5g carbohydrate; 11.3g protein; 6.5g fibre

spinach and zucchini salad with yogurt hummus

½ cup (100g) dried chickpeas
1 small zucchini (90g), sliced thickly
1 clove garlic, unpeeled
2 tablespoons fresh lemon juice
2 teaspoons tahini
1 tablespoon goat milk yogurt
60g baby spinach leaves
½ small red onion (50g), sliced thinly

1   Place chickpeas in small bowl, cover with water; stand overnight,
drain. Rinse under cold water; drain.
2   Cook chickpeas in small saucepan of boiling water, uncovered,
until just tender; drain over small bowl, reserve 2 teaspoons of the
liquid. Rinse chickpeas under cold water; drain.
3   Meanwhile, cook zucchini and garlic on heated lightly oiled grill
plate (or grill or barbecue) until browned both sides. When cool
enough to handle, peel garlic.
4   Blend or process ¼ cup cooked chickpeas, juice, tahini, yogurt,
reserved liquid and garlic until smooth.
5   Place spinach, onion and remaining chickpeas in medium bowl;
toss gently to combine.
6   Serve salad drizzled with yogurt hummus.
preparation time 25 minutes (plus standing time)
cooking time 30 minutes **serves** 1
nutritional count per serving 14.6g total fat (2.3g saturated fat);
1701kJ (407 cal); 43.4g carbohydrate; 24.3g protein; 18.8g fibre

greek salad

spinach and zucchini salad with yogurt hummus

potato and bean salad with lemon yogurt dressing   pan-fried tofu with vietnamese coleslaw salad

potato and bean salad with lemon yogurt dressing

2 small potatoes (240g), unpeeled,
   cut into wedges
150g green beans, trimmed,
   cut into 3cm lengths
1 cup (230g) baby rocket leaves
½ small red onion (50g), sliced thinly
lemon yogurt dressing
⅓ cup (95g) sheep milk yogurt
1 teaspoon finely grated lemon rind
1 tablespoon fresh lemon juice
1 tablespoon finely chopped
   fresh flat-leaf parsley

1 Boil, steam or microwave potato and beans, separately, until tender; drain. Rinse beans under cold water; drain.
2 Meanwhile, combine ingredients for lemon yogurt dressing in small bowl.
3 Place potato and beans in medium bowl with rocket and onion; toss gently to combine. Serve salad drizzled with dressing.
preparation time 15 minutes cooking time 15 minutes serves 1
nutritional count per serving 6.6g total fat (1g saturated fat); 1308kJ (313 cal); 43.9g carbohydrate; 15.2g protein; 10.3g fibre

pan-fried tofu with vietnamese coleslaw salad

100g firm silken tofu
1 small carrot (70g)
½ cup (40g) finely shredded
   green cabbage
½ cup (40g) finely shredded
   red cabbage
½ small yellow capsicum (75g),
   sliced thinly
½ cup (40g) bean sprouts
2 green onions, sliced thinly
¼ cup loosely packed fresh
   coriander leaves
lime and garlic dressing
¼ cup (60ml) fresh lime juice
1 clove garlic, crushed

1 Place tofu, in single layer, on absorbent-paper-lined tray; cover tofu with more absorbent paper, stand 10 minutes.
2 Meanwhile, using vegetable peeler, slice carrot into ribbons. Place in medium bowl with cabbages, capsicum, sprouts, onion and coriander; toss gently to combine.
3 Place ingredients for lime and garlic dressing in screw-top jar; shake well.
4 Cut tofu into four slices; cook tofu in heated lightly oiled small frying pan until browned both sides.
5 Drizzle dressing over salad; serve with tofu.
preparation time 20 minutes cooking time 5 minutes serves 1
nutritional count per serving 7.4g total fat (1g saturated fat); 798kJ (191 cal); 11.9g carbohydrate; 17.5g protein; 10.3g fibre

big salads

pearl barley salad

½ cup (100g) pearl barley
125g asparagus, trimmed,
    cut into 4cm lengths
125g cherry tomatoes, halved
½ lebanese cucumber (65g), sliced thinly
¾ cup (45g) finely shredded
    iceberg lettuce
2 tablespoons coarsely chopped
    fresh basil
2 tablespoons fresh lemon juice

1   Cook barley in small saucepan of boiling water, uncovered, about 25 minutes or until tender; drain. Cool 10 minutes.
2   Meanwhile, boil, steam or microwave asparagus until just tender; drain.
3   Place barley and asparagus in medium bowl with remaining ingredients; toss gently to combine.

preparation time 10 minutes **cooking time** 25 minutes **serves** 1
nutritional count per serving 2.9g total fat (0.4g saturated fat); 1513kJ (362 cal); 68.4g carbohydrate; 13.5g protein; 17g fibre

cos, snow pea and roasted celeriac salad

100g celeriac, chopped coarsely
4 cloves garlic, unpeeled
cooking-oil spray
50g baby green beans, trimmed,
    chopped coarsely
2 tablespoons fresh lemon juice
2 teaspoons walnut oil
½ baby cos lettuce (90g), torn
50g snow peas, trimmed, sliced thinly
½ cup (50g) toasted walnuts,
    chopped coarsely

1   Preheat oven to 240°C/220°C fan-forced.
2   Place celeriac and garlic on shallow oven tray; spray with oil. Roast, uncovered, 20 minutes or until celeriac is just tender and garlic softens.
3   Meanwhile, boil, steam or microwave beans until tender; drain. Rinse under cold water; drain.
4   When garlic is cool enough to handle, squeeze garlic from skins into screw-top jar. Add juice and oil; shake well.
5   Place celeriac and beans in medium bowl with lettuce, snow peas, nuts and dressing; toss gently to combine.

preparation time 15 minutes **cooking time** 20 minutes **serves** 1
nutritional count per serving 46.9g total fat (13.2g saturated fat); 2215kJ (530 cal); 14g carbohydrate; 13.7g protein; 14.1g fibre

pearl barley salad

cos, snow pea and roasted celeriac salad

chickpea, watercress and capsicum salad

potato and asparagus salad with yogurt and mint dressing

chickpea, watercress and capsicum salad

¼ cup (50g) dried chickpeas
100g watercress
1 tablespoon water
1 clove garlic, quartered
¼ cup (35g) toasted slivered almonds
¼ cup (60ml) fresh lemon juice
⅓ small red capsicum (50g), sliced thinly
⅓ small yellow capsicum (50g),
   sliced thinly

1 Place chickpeas in small bowl, cover with water; stand overnight, drain. Rinse under cold water; drain.
2 Cook chickpeas in small saucepan of boiling water, uncovered, until just tender; drain. Rinse under cold water; drain.
3 Trim watercress; reserve stalks. Blend or process watercress stalks with the water, garlic, a third of the chickpeas, 1 tablespoon of the nuts and 2 tablespoons of the juice until smooth. Transfer to medium bowl; stir in remaining chickpeas and remaining nuts.
4 Place watercress leaves and capsicums in medium bowl with remaining juice; toss gently to combine. Top with chickpea mixture.
preparation time 15 minutes (plus standing time)
cooking time 30 minutes **serves** 1
nutritional count per serving 21.4g total fat (1.5g saturated fat); 1371kJ (328 cal); 15.8g carbohydrate; 16g protein; 11.4g fibre

potato and asparagus salad with yogurt and mint dressing

150g baby new potatoes, unpeeled
125g asparagus, trimmed,
   cut into 3cm lengths
½ lebanese cucumber (65g), sliced thinly
40g watercress, trimmed
¼ cup (40g) toasted pepitas
yogurt and mint dressing
2 tablespoons sheep milk yogurt
1 teaspoon finely grated lime rind
2 teaspoons fresh lime juice
¼ cup finely chopped fresh mint

1 Boil, steam or microwave potatoes until tender; drain. When cool enough to handle, quarter potatoes.
2 Meanwhile, boil, steam or microwave asparagus until tender; drain. Rinse under cold water; drain.
3 Combine ingredients for yogurt and mint dressing in small bowl.
4 Place potato and asparagus in medium bowl with cucumber, watercress, pepitas and dressing; toss gently to combine.
preparation time 20 minutes **cooking time** 20 minutes **serves** 1
nutritional count per serving 16.8g total fat (1g saturated fat); 1672kJ (400 cal); 25.7g carbohydrate; 10.7g protein; 11.8g fibre

roasted egg tomatoes with barley salad

¼ cup (50g) pearl barley
2 medium egg tomatoes (150g),
   cut into thick wedges
1 small green capsicum (150g),
   chopped finely
½ small red onion (50g), chopped finely
½ cup coarsely chopped fresh
   flat-leaf parsley
lemon and dill dressing
2 tablespoons fresh lemon juice
1 tablespoon finely chopped fresh dill
1 teaspoon olive oil
1 clove garlic, crushed

1 Preheat oven to 240°C/220°C fan-forced.
2 Cook barley in small saucepan of boiling water, uncovered, about 20 minutes or until just tender; drain. Rinse under cold water; drain.
3 Meanwhile, place tomato, cut-side up, on lightly oiled oven tray. Roast tomato, uncovered, about 15 minutes or until just softened.
4 Place ingredients for lemon and dill dressing in screw-top jar; shake well.
5 Place barley and half of the tomato in medium bowl with capsicum, onion, parsley and dressing; toss gently to combine. Top with remaining tomato.

preparation time 15 minutes **cooking time** 20 minutes **serves** 1
nutritional count per serving 6.4g total fat (0.9g saturated fat); 1191kJ (285 cal); 44.4g carbohydrate; 10.7g protein; 13.4g fibre

borlotti bean, brown rice and almond salad

¼ cup (50g) dried borlotti beans
¼ cup (50g) brown long-grain rice
½ small red onion (50g), chopped finely
¼ cup finely chopped fresh
   flat-leaf parsley
¼ cup finely chopped fresh mint
1 medium tomato (150g), chopped finely
1 tablespoon roasted slivered almonds
2 tablespoons fresh lemon juice
2 teaspoons olive oil

1 Place beans in small bowl, cover with water; stand overnight, drain. Rinse under cold water; drain.
2 Cook beans in small saucepan of boiling water, uncovered, until just tender; drain. Rinse under cold water; drain.
3 Meanwhile, cook rice in small saucepan of boiling water, uncovered, until rice is tender; drain. Rinse under cold water; drain.
4 Place beans and rice in medium bowl with remaining ingredients; toss gently to combine.

preparation time 10 minutes (plus standing time)
cooking time 20 minutes **serves** 1
nutritional count per serving 18.4g total fat (2.1g saturated fat); 2140kJ (512 cal); 63.4g carbohydrate; 21.3g protein; 13.4g fibre

roasted egg tomatoes with barley salad

borlotti bean, brown rice and almond salad

thai soy bean salad with grapes and pink grapefruit

pear, spinach, walnut and celery salad

thai soy bean salad with grapes and pink grapefruit

¼ cup (50g) dried soya beans
1 small pink grapefruit (350g),
   segmented
50g green grapes, halved
1 small white onion (80g),
   chopped finely
50g snow pea sprouts, trimmed
¼ cup finely chopped fresh coriander
¼ cup finely chopped fresh mint
1 fresh kaffir lime leaf, shredded finely
2 tablespoons fresh lime juice

1 Place beans in small bowl, cover with water; stand overnight, drain. Rinse under cold water; drain.
2 Cook beans in small saucepan of boiling water, uncovered, until just tender; drain. Rinse under cold water; drain.
3 Place beans in medium bowl with remaining ingredients; toss gently to combine

preparation time 15 minutes (plus standing time)
cooking time 20 minutes **serves** 1
nutritional count per serving 11.3g total fat (1.6g saturated fat); 1517kJ (363 cal); 38.3g carbohydrate; 24.6g protein; 16.9g fibre

pear, spinach, walnut and celery salad

1 large pear (330g), cut into thin wedges
60g baby spinach leaves
¼ cup (25g) toasted walnuts,
   chopped coarsely
1 trimmed celery stalk (100g),
   chopped coarsely
mustard dressing
2 teaspoons american mustard
1 teaspoon cider vinegar
1 tablespoon fresh apple juice

1 Place ingredients for mustard dressing in screw-top jar; shake well.
2 Place pear, spinach, nuts and celery in medium bowl; toss gently to combine.
3 Serve salad drizzled with dressing.

preparation time 10 minutes **serves** 1
nutritional count per serving 18.1g total fat (1.1g saturated fat); 1601kJ (383 cal); 50.5g carbohydrate; 6.9g protein; 12.1g fibre

big salads

grilled asparagus with warm tomato dressing

1 medium tomato (150g), chopped finely
1 clove garlic, crushed
2 tablespoons fresh lemon juice
1 tablespoon finely chopped fresh basil
1 tablespoon finely chopped fresh
    flat-leaf parsley
125g asparagus, trimmed
25g curly endive, torn
25g rocket leaves

1 Combine tomato, garlic and juice in small saucepan; bring to the boil. Reduce heat; simmer, uncovered, 2 minutes. Remove from heat; stir in herbs.

2 Meanwhile, cook asparagus on heated lightly oiled grill plate (or grill or barbecue) until just tender.

3 Place endive and rocket on medium serving plate; top with asparagus and tomato mixture.

preparation time 20 minutes **cooking time** 15 minutes **serves** 1
nutritional count per serving 0.7g total fat (0g saturated fat); 272kJ (65 cal); 6.7g carbohydrate; 6.3g protein; 6.5g fibre

soba salad with seaweed, ginger and vegetables

5g wakame
50g soba noodles
1 lebanese cucumber (130g), seeded,
    cut into matchsticks
1 small carrot (70g), cut into matchsticks
1 tablespoon toasted sesame seeds
1 green onion, sliced thinly
1cm piece fresh ginger (5g), grated
1 teaspoon sesame oil
2 tablespoons fresh lime juice
1 teaspoon tamari

1 Place wakame in small bowl, cover with cold water; stand 10 minutes or until wakame softens, drain. Discard any hard stems; chop coarsely.

2 Meanwhile, cook soba in small saucepan of boiling water, uncovered, until just tender; drain. Rinse under cold water; drain. Chop soba coarsely.

3 Place wakame and soba in medium bowl with remaining ingredients; toss gently to combine.

preparation time 10 minutes **cooking time** 5 minutes **serves** 1
nutritional count per serving 12.2g total fat (1.6g saturated fat); 1367kJ (327 cal); 41.5g carbohydrate; 11.1g protein; 9.1g fibre
tips Wakame, a bright green seaweed usually sold in dried form, is used in soups, salads and seasonings. Dried wakame must be softened by soaking for about 10 minutes, and any hard stems are then discarded.
It is available from most Asian food stores. Soba is a Japanese noodle, similar in appearance to spaghetti, made from buckwheat.

grilled asparagus with warm tomato dressing

soba salad with seaweed, ginger and vegetables

tomato and avocado salad with tofu pesto

roasted pumpkin, pecan and fetta salad

tomato and avocado salad with tofu pesto

1 medium tomato (150g),
    cut into wedges
½ medium avocado (125g), sliced thickly
100g firm silken tofu, diced into
    3cm pieces
50g mesclun
1 tablespoon fresh basil leaves
tofu pesto
1 tablespoon toasted pine nuts
50g firm tofu
½ cup firmly packed fresh basil leaves
1 tablespoon fresh lemon juice
1 tablespoon water

1 Blend or process ingredients for tofu pesto until smooth.
2 Combine salad ingredients in medium bowl; serve salad topped with pesto.
preparation time 10 minutes serves 1
nutritional count per serving 40.6g total fat (6.4g saturated fat); 2044kJ (489 cal); 7g carbohydrate; 24g protein; 8.6g fibre

roasted pumpkin, pecan and fetta salad

100g pumpkin, chopped coarsely
cooking-oil spray
80g rocket leaves
⅓ cup (40g) toasted pecans
50g goat fetta cheese, crumbled
citrus dressing
1 tablespoon fresh orange juice
1 tablespoon fresh lemon juice
1 teaspoon grapeseed oil

1 Preheat oven to 240°C/220°C fan-forced.
2 Place pumpkin on lightly oiled oven tray; spray with oil. Roast, uncovered, about 20 minutes or until tender.
3 Place ingredients for citrus dressing in screw-top jar; shake well.
4 Combine pumpkin in medium bowl with remaining ingredients and dressing; toss gently to combine.
preparation time 15 minutes cooking time 20 minutes serves 1
nutritional count per serving 44.3g total fat (7.9g saturated fat); 2111kJ (505 cal); 12.7g carbohydrate; 14.9g protein; 5.8g fibre

big salads

baked beetroot salad
with cannellini beans, fetta and mint

¼ cup (50g) dried cannellini beans
1 medium beetroot (175g),
   diced into 3cm pieces
cooking-oil spray
50g goat fetta cheese, crumbled
50g mesclun
¼ cup loosely packed fresh mint leaves
apple dressing
2 tablespoons fresh apple juice
2 teaspoons american mustard

1 Place beans in small bowl, cover with water; stand overnight, drain. Rinse under cold water; drain.

2 Cook beans in small saucepan of boiling water, uncovered, until just tender; drain. Rinse under cold water; drain.

3 Preheat oven to 200°C/180°C fan-forced.

4 Place beetroot in small shallow baking dish; spray with oil. Bake, covered, about 20 minutes or until tender.

5 Place ingredients for apple dressing in screw-top jar; shake well.

6 Place beans and beetroot in medium bowl with remaining ingredients and dressing; toss gently to combine.

preparation time 10 minutes (plus standing time)
cooking time 50 minutes **serves** 1
nutritional count per serving 10.3g total fat (5.4g saturated fat); 1417kJ (339 cal); 39.4g carbohydrate; 21.7g protein; 16.3g fibre

big salads

109

apple and pear compote with dates

1 small apple (130g)
1 small pear (180g)
2 tablespoons fresh lemon juice
⅓ cup (55g) coarsely chopped
   dried dates
1 teaspoon finely grated orange rind
2 tablespoons fresh orange juice

1 Peel and core apple and pear; dice into 2cm pieces. Combine apple and pear in small saucepan with lemon juice; cook, covered, over low heat, about 10 minutes or until fruit softens.
2 Meanwhile, combine dates, rind and orange juice in small saucepan; cook, uncovered, over low heat, stirring occasionally, about 5 minutes or until liquid is absorbed.
3 Serve compote, warm or cold, topped with date mixture and finely shredded orange rind, if desired.

preparation time 5 minutes **cooking time** 10 minutes **serves** 1
nutritional count per serving 0.5g total fat (0g saturated fat); 1242kJ (297 cal); 72.1g carbohydrate; 2.4g protein; 9.9g fibre

fruit dishes

macerated fruits

¼ cup (20g) dried apples
¼ cup (35g) dried apricots
½ cup (125ml) fresh apple juice
2 teaspoons fresh lemon juice

1 Combine ingredients in small bowl.
2 Cover; refrigerate 2 hours or overnight.
preparation time 5 minutes (plus refrigeration time)
serves 1 **nutritional count per serving** 0.2g total fat
(0g saturated fat); 723kJ (173 cal); 41.4g carbohydrate;
1.9g protein; 5g fibre

four-fruit combo

1 small pear (180g), chopped coarsely
1 small apple (130g), chopped coarsely
1 small pink grapefruit (350g), segmented
100g red grapes

1 Combine ingredients in medium bowl.
preparation time 10 minutes **serves** 1
nutritional count per serving 0.8g total fat
(0g saturated fat); 1066kJ (255 cal);
58.5g carbohydrate; 4.1g protein; 8.1g fibre

papaya with passionfruit and lime

We used the red-fleshed Hawaiian or Fijian variety instead of the yellow-fleshed papaya here. You need one passionfruit for this recipe.

1 small papaya (650g), cut into thick wedges
1 tablespoon fresh passionfruit pulp
2 teaspoons fresh lime juice

1   Place papaya on medium serving plate.
2   Drizzle with passionfruit and juice.
preparation time 10 minutes **serves** 1
nutritional count per serving 0.5g total fat
(0g saturated fat); 598kJ (143 cal); 32.3g carbohydrate;
2.5g protein; 13.1g fibre

banana with passionfruit yogurt

You need two passionfruits for this recipe.

2 tablespoons sheep milk yogurt
2 tablespoons fresh passionfruit pulp
1 medium banana (200g), sliced thickly

1   Combine yogurt and half of the passionfruit in small bowl.
2   Place banana in small bowl; top with yogurt mixture and remaining passionfruit.
preparation time 5 minutes **serves** 1
nutritional count per serving 3.1g total fat
(0g saturated fat); 757kJ (181 cal); 31.2g carbohydrate;
5.6g protein; 8.5g fibre

fruit dishes

113

figs with sheep milk yogurt and honey

2 medium fresh figs (120g), chopped coarsely
¼ cup (70g) sheep milk yogurt
4 medium fresh figs (240g), halved
1 teaspoon honey

1 Combine chopped figs and yogurt in small bowl.
2 Place halved figs on serving plate; drizzle with honey.
3 Serve with yogurt mixture.
preparation time 5 minutes **serves** 1
nutritional count per serving 5.2g total fat
(0g saturated fat); 932kJ (223 cal); 35.2g carbohydrate;
7.5g protein; 6.8g fibre

kiwi fruit, lychee and lime salad

2 kiwi fruits (170g), cut into wedges
4 fresh lychees (100g)
1 tablespoon fresh mint leaves
1 tablespoon fresh lime juice

1 Combine ingredients in small bowl.
preparation time 5 minutes **serves** 1
nutritional count per serving 0.5g total fat
(0g saturated fat); 535kJ (128 cal); 26.8g carbohydrate;
3.2g protein; 6.1g fibre

lychees with passionfruit

banana with passionfruit

You need two passionfruit for this recipe.

You need one passionfruit for this recipe.

20 fresh lychees (500g)
2 tablespoons fresh passionfruit pulp

2 medium bananas (400g)
1 tablespoon fresh passionfruit pulp

1 Blend or process half of the lychees until smooth; stir in half of the passionfruit.
2 Place remaining lychees in small bowl; top with lychee mixture and remaining passionfruit.
preparation time 5 minutes **serves** 1
nutritional count per serving 0.4g total fat (0g saturated fat); 1112kJ (266 cal); 62g carbohydrate; 4.8g protein; 7.8g fibre

1 Cut bananas in half lengthways; cut each half into two pieces.
2 Place banana in medium serving bowl; drizzle with passionfruit pulp.
preparation time 5 minutes **serves** 1
nutritional count per serving 0.3g total fat (0g saturated fat); 999kJ (239 cal); 54.5g carbohydrate; 5.2g protein; 8.8g fibre

fruit dishes

stewed prunes with orange

½ cup (85g) seeded dried prunes
¼ cup (60ml) fresh orange juice
¼ cup (60ml) water
5cm strip orange rind, sliced thinly
1 cinnamon stick
2 cardamon pods, bruised

1   Place ingredients in small saucepan; bring to the boil. Reduce heat; simmer, covered, 10 minutes.
2   Serve stewed prunes with sheep milk yogurt, if desired.
preparation time 5 minutes
cooking time 15 minutes **serves** 1
nutritional count per serving 0.4g total fat
(0g saturated fat); 752kJ (180 cal); 42.2g carbohydrate; 2.3g protein; 6.8g fibre

mango cheeks with lime wedges

1 large mango (600g)
½ lime, cut into wedges

1   Slice cheeks from mango; score each cheek in shallow criss-cross pattern, taking care not to cut through skin.
2   Serve mango cheeks with lime wedges.
preparation time 5 minutes **serves** 1
nutritional count per serving 1g total fat
(0g saturated fat); 1074kJ (257 cal); 54.6g carbohydrate; 4.9g protein; 8g fibre

cherries and yogurt

1½ cups (225g) cherries
⅓ cup (95g) sheep milk yogurt

1 Place cherries on small serving plate; serve with yogurt.
preparation time 5 minutes **serves** 1
nutritional count per serving 6g total fat
(0g saturated fat); 23.4g carbohydrate; 757kJ (181 cal)
6g protein; 2.7g fibre

blood plums with honey and cardamom yogurt

¼ cup (70g) sheep milk yogurt
2 teaspoons honey
¼ teaspoon ground cardamom
2 small blood plums (180g), quartered

1 Combine yogurt, honey and cardamom in small bowl.
2 Place plums on small serving plate; drizzle with yogurt mixture.
preparation time 5 minutes **serves** 1
nutritional count per serving 4.4g total fat
(0g saturated fat); 26.7g carbohydrate; 732kJ (175 cal);
4.2g protein; 3.6g fibre

fruit dishes

hot grapefruit water

3½ cups (875ml) boiling water
½ cup (125ml) fresh grapefruit juice

1 Place the water in large jug; stir in juice.
preparation time 5 minutes **makes** 1 litre
nutritional count per 250ml 0g total fat
(0g saturated fat); 33kJ (8 cal); 1.5g carbohydrate;
0.3g protein; 0.4g fibre

hot lemon water

3½ cups (875ml) boiling water
½ cup (125ml) fresh lemon juice

1 Place the water in large jug; stir in juice.
2 Serve with lemon slices, if desired.
preparation time 5 minutes **makes** 1 litre
nutritional count per 250ml 0.1g total fat
(0g saturated fat); 38kJ (9 cal); 0.9g carbohydrate;
0.2g protein; 0g fibre

drinks & nightcaps

centre hot grapefruit water **right** hot lemon water

left lemon grass and kaffir lime tea **centre** cardamom and chamomile tea **right** almond milk

lemon grass and kaffir lime tea

10cm stick fresh lemon grass (20g), chopped finely
4 fresh kaffir lime leaves
1 litre (4 cups) water

1 Combine ingredients in small saucepan; bring to the boil.
2 Reduce heat; simmer, uncovered, about 5 minutes. Cool 5 minutes; strain.
preparation time 5 minutes **cooking time** 10 minutes
makes 1 litre **nutritional count per 250ml** 0g total fat (0g saturated fat); 1kJ (0.3 cal); 0g carbohydrate; 0g protein; 0g fibre

cardamom and chamomile tea

2 tablespoons loose-leafed chamomile tea
4 cardamom pods, bruised
1 litre (4 cups) water

1 Combine ingredients in small saucepan; bring to the boil.
2 Reduce heat; simmer, uncovered, about 5 minutes. Cool 5 minutes; strain.
preparation time 5 minutes **cooking time** 10 minutes
makes 1 litre **nutritional count per 250ml** 0g total fat (0g saturated fat); 0.6kJ (0.2 cal); 0g carbohydrate; 0g protein; 0g fibre

almond milk

1 cup (250ml) water
½ cup (70g) roasted slivered almonds
3 drops vanilla extract

1 Blend or process the water and nuts until pureed.
2 Strain mixture through muslin-lined sieve into small jug; discard solids. Add extract; stir to combine. Refrigerate until chilled.
preparation time 5 minutes (plus refrigeration time)
makes ¾ cup
nutritional count per 180ml 38.1g total fat (3.8g saturated fat); 1697kJ (406 cal); 3.1g carbohydrate; 14.3g protein; 6.3g fibre

cinnamon and orange tea

2 cinnamon sticks
10cm strip orange rind
1 litre (4 cups) water

1 Combine ingredients in small saucepan; bring to the boil.
2 Reduce heat; simmer, uncovered, about 5 minutes. Cool 5 minutes; strain.
preparation time 5 minutes **cooking time** 10 minutes **makes** 1 litre **nutritional count per 250ml** 0g total fat (0g saturated fat); 13kJ (3 cal); 0.6g carbohydrate; 0.1g protein; 0.2g fibre

mint tea

½ cup coarsely chopped fresh mint
1 litre (4 cups) boiling water

1 Combine ingredients in large heatproof jug.
2 Stand, uncovered, 3 minutes; strain.
preparation time 5 minutes **makes** 1 litre **nutritional count per 250ml** 0.1g total fat (0g saturated fat); 13kJ (3 cal); 0.3g carbohydrate; 0.2g protein; 0.5g fibre
tip Any unused tea can be reheated in a microwave oven or served chilled.

ginger tea

20cm piece fresh ginger (100g), sliced thinly
1.5 litres (6 cups) water

1 Combine ingredients in medium saucepan; bring to the boil.
2 Reduce heat; simmer, uncovered, about 15 minutes or until liquid has reduced by a third. Cool 5 minutes; strain.
preparation time 5 minutes **cooking time** 20 minutes **makes** 1 litre **nutritional count per 250ml** 0.1g total fat (0g saturated fat); 29kJ (7 cal); 1g carbohydrate; 0.2g protein; 0.7g fibre
tip Any unused tea can be reheated in a microwave oven or served chilled.

left cinnamon and orange tea **centre** mint tea **right** ginger tea

glossary

almonds
flaked paper-thin slices.
slivered small lengthways-cut pieces.
bamboo shoots tender shoots of
bamboo plants, available in cans;
drain and rinse before use.
barley a nutritious grain; hulled
barley is the least processed form
of barley and is high in fibre. Pearl
barley has had the husk discarded
then hulled and polished, like rice.
bay leaves aromatic leaves from
the bay tree used for flavouring.
beans
black-eyed also known as black-
eyed peas.
borlotti also known as roman beans;
can be eaten fresh or dried.
green sometimes called french or
string beans, this long fresh bean is
consumed pod and all.
yellow string also called wax, french,
runner and, incorrectly, butter beans;
a yellow-coloured fresh green bean.
beetroot also called red beets or just
beets; firm, round root vegetable.
broccolini a cross between broccoli
and chinese kale; long asparagus-
like stems with a loose floret, both
completely edible. Resembles
broccoli in look but is milder and
sweeter in taste. Substitute with gai
lan or common broccoli.
buk choy also called bak choy,
pak choi, chinese white cabbage or
chinese chard; has a mild mustard
taste. Use stems and leaves. Baby
buk choy is smaller and more tender.
capsicum also called bell pepper.
cardamom available in pod, seed
or ground form. Has a distinctive
aromatic, sweetly rich flavour.

celeriac tuberous root with brown
skin, white flesh and celery-like flavour.
cheese
fetta crumbly goat- or sheep-milk
cheese having a sharp salty taste.
goat made from goat milk, has an
earthy, strong taste. Available soft and
firm, and in various shapes and sizes.
ricotta soft white cow milk cheese;
roughly translates as "cooked again".
Is a slightly grainy, sweet, moist cheese
with a fat content of around 8.5%.
chickpeas also called garbanzos,
hummus or channa; an irregularly
round, sandy-coloured legume.
cinnamon stick the dried inner bark
of the shoots of the cinnamon tree.
curly endive also known as frisee, a
curly-leafed green vegetable, mainly
used in salads.
currants dried, tiny, almost black
raisins named after a grape variety
that originated in Corinth, Greece.
fennel also known as finocchio or
anise. Also the name given to dried
seeds having a licorice flavour.
gai lan also known as gai lum,
kanah, or chinese kale; appreciated
more for its stems than its coarse
leaves. Available from Asian food
stores and many greengrocers.
ginger also known as green or root
ginger; the thick gnarled root of a
tropical plant. Cannot be substituted
with ginger powder.
juice, fresh we made our own fresh
juice in every recipe.
kaffir lime leaves also known as bai
magrood; glossy dark green leaves
joined end to end to form a rounded

hourglass shape. Sold fresh, dried or
frozen; dried leaves are less potent
so double the number called for if
you substitute them for fresh leaves.
A strip of fresh lime peel can be
substituted for each kaffir lime leaf.
kumara Polynesian name of orange-
fleshed sweet potato often confused
with yam.
lemon grass a tall, clumping,
lemon-smelling and tasting, sharp-
edged grass; the white lower part
of each stem is finely chopped and
used in Asian cooking or for tea.
lentils (red, brown, yellow) dried
pulses often identified by and named
after their colour.
french green originally from France,
these are a small, dark-green, fast-
cooking lentils with a delicate flavour.
lychees a fruit with a light texture
and flavour; peel away rough skin
and remove seed. Available in cans.
mandarin a small, loose-skinned
citrus fruit. Segments in a light syrup
are available canned.
mango tropical fruit with skin colour
ranging from green through yellow
to deep red. Mango cheeks in a light
syrup are available canned.
mesclun mixed baby salad leaves
also sold as salad mix or gourmet
salad mix; a mixture of assorted
young lettuce and other green leaves.
mushrooms
button small, cultivated mushrooms
with a delicate, subtle flavour.
oyster also called abalone; a grey-
white mushroom shaped like a fan.
Has a subtle, oyster-like flavour.

portobello are mature swiss browns. These large, dark brown mushrooms have a robust, full-bodied flavour.
shiitake when fresh are also known as chinese black, forest or golden oak mushrooms; although cultivated, they have an earthy taste. When dried, are known as donko or dried chinese mushrooms; rehydrate before use.
swiss brown light to dark brown mushrooms with full-bodied flavour. Use button or cup mushrooms.
oil
grapeseed made from grape seeds. Available from most supermarkets.
olive made from ripened olives. Extra virgin and virgin are the first and second press, respectively, of the olives, while extra light or light refers to taste, not fat levels.
peanut pressed from ground peanuts; has high smoke point (capacity to handle high heat without burning).
sesame made from roasted, crushed white sesame seeds.
walnut made from walnuts.
onions
green also called scallion or, incorrectly, shallot; an immature onion picked before the bulb has formed. Has a bright-green edible stalk.
red also known as red spanish, spanish or bermuda onion; a sweet-flavoured, large, purple-red onion.
shallots also called french shallots, golden shallots or eschalots; small, elongated and brown-skinned. Grows in tight clusters similar to garlic.
spring small white bulbs, long green leaves and narrow green-leafed tops.

papaya a large, pear-shaped red-orange tropical fruit. Sometimes used unripened (green) in cooking.
pepitas dried pumpkin seeds.
pine nuts also known as pignoli; not, in fact, a nut, but a small, cream-coloured kernel from pine cones.
pistachios pale green, delicately flavoured nut inside hard, off-white shell.
polenta also known as cornmeal; a flour-like cereal made of dried corn (maize) sold ground; also the name of the dish made from it.
radicchio a member of the chicory family. Has dark burgundy leaves and a strong bitter flavour.
rocket also known as arugula, rugula and rucola; a peppery-tasting green leaf that can be eaten raw or used in cooking. Baby rocket leaves are both smaller and less peppery.
rolled oats husked, steam-softened, flattened and dried oats.
sesame seeds black and white are the most common. Toast briefly in moderate oven.
silver beet also called swiss chard. A green-leafed vegetable with sturdy celery-like white stems.
soba noodles thin spaghetti-like pale brown noodle from Japan made from buckwheat and wheat flour.
spinach also known as english spinach and, incorrectly, silver beet.
split peas also known as field peas; a green or yellow pulse.
sunflower seeds kernels from dried husked sunflower seeds.
swedes also known as rutabaga; a yellow skin, looks similar to turnips.

tahini sesame seed paste; available from Middle-Eastern food stores.
tamari a thick, dark sauce made from soy beans with a distinctive mellow flavour. Available from most supermarkets and Asian food stores.
tangelo cross between a grapefruit and tangerine; a loose-skinned, juicy, sweetly-tart citrus fruit with few seeds. Is eaten like an orange.
tofu also called bean curd, an off-white, custard-like product made from the milk of crushed soy beans.
tomato
cherry also known as tiny tim or tom thumb, small and round.
egg smallish and oval-shaped; also called plum or roma.
turmeric also known as kamin; related to galangal and ginger. Must be grated or pounded to release its acrid aroma and pungent flavour.
vinegar, cider made from fermented apples.
wakame a bright-green seaweed, usually sold in dry form; available from Asian food stores. Soak in water for 10 minutes; discard hard stems.
walnuts a rich, flavourful nut. Store in the refrigerator because of its high oil content.
watercress a highly perishable peppery greens, use as soon as possible after purchase.
wombok also known as chinese cabbage; elongated in shape with pale green, crinkly leaves.
yogurt we used either sheep- or goat-milk yogurt in this book.
zucchini also called courgette.

index

index

127

conversion chart

measures

One Australian metric measuring cup holds approximately 250ml; one Australian metric tablespoon holds 20ml; one Australian metric teaspoon holds 5ml.

The difference between one country's measuring cups and another's is within a two- or three-teaspoon variance, and will not affect your cooking results. North America, New Zealand and the United Kingdom use a 15ml tablespoon.

All cup and spoon measurements are level. The most accurate way of measuring dry ingredients is to weigh them. When measuring liquids, use a clear glass or plastic jug with the metric markings.

We use large eggs with an average weight of 60g.

dry measures

METRIC	IMPERIAL
15g	½oz
30g	1oz
60g	2oz
90g	3oz
125g	4oz (¼lb)
155g	5oz
185g	6oz
220g	7oz
250g	8oz (½lb)
280g	9oz
315g	10oz
345g	11oz
375g	12oz (¾lb)
410g	13oz
440g	14oz
470g	15oz
500g	16oz (1lb)
750g	24oz (1½lb)
1kg	32oz (2lb)

liquid measures

METRIC	IMPERIAL
30ml	1 fluid oz
60ml	2 fluid oz
100ml	3 fluid oz
125ml	4 fluid oz
150ml	5 fluid oz (¼ pint/1 gill)
190ml	6 fluid oz
250ml	8 fluid oz
300ml	10 fluid oz (½ pint)
500ml	16 fluid oz
600ml	20 fluid oz (1 pint)
1000ml (1 litre)	1¾ pints

length measures

3mm	⅛in
6mm	¼in
1cm	½in
2cm	¾in
2.5cm	1in
5cm	2in
6cm	2½in
8cm	3in
10cm	4in
13cm	5in
15cm	6in
18cm	7in
20cm	8in
23cm	9in
25cm	10in
28cm	11in
30cm	12in (1ft)

oven temperatures

These oven temperatures are only a guide for conventional ovens. For fan-forced ovens, check the manufacturer's manual.

	°C (CELSIUS)	°F (FAHRENHEIT)	GAS MARK
Very slow	120	250	½
Slow	150	275-300	1-2
Moderately slow	160	325	3
Moderate	180	350-375	4-5
Moderately hot	200	400	6
Hot	220	425-450	7-8
Very hot	240	475	9